Choosing Schools: Parents, LEAs and the 1980 Education Act

Andy Stillman and
Karen Maychell

NFER-NELSON

Published by The NFER-NELSON Publishing Company Ltd.,
Darville House, 2 Oxford Road East,
Windsor, Berkshire SL4 1DF, England

and in the United States of America by

NFER-NELSON, 242 Cherry Street, Philadelphia, PA 19106 – 1906.
Tel: (215) 238 0939.   Telex: 244489.

First Published 1986
© 1986 National Foundation for Educational Research

Library of Congress Cataloging in Publication data

Stillman, Andy.
   Choosing Schools.

   Bibliography: p.

   1.   School, Choice of — Great Britain. 2.   High schools — Great Britain
— Admission. 3.   School boards — Great Britain. 4.   Students, Transfer
of — Great Britain. 5.   Educational law and legislation — Great Britain.
I.   Maychell, Karen. II.   Title.
LB3064.4.G6S55 1986   373.12'1   86–8547
ISBN 0–7005–1069–9

Photoset in Times by David John (Services) Ltd., Maidenhead, Berks.

Printed in Great Britain by A. Wheaton & Co. Ltd, Exeter

ISBN 0–7005–1069–9
Code 8247 02 1

W 32406 [9.95. 11.86

Contents

Preface

The Information for Parental Choice Project commenced in July 1983 and continued until June 1985. The research, which was sponsored by the National Foundation for Educational Research, had three main aims:

1   To discover the range of theoretical and real choice open to parents when their children transfer to secondary school;

2   To investigate the procedures adopted by schools and LEAs to inform parents of what they offer and how to exercise their right to express a preference;

3   To identify the factors which influence parental decisions when their children transfer to secondary school.

Whilst an investigation of parental choice issues might be considered relevant at any time, the implementation in 1982 of the 1980 Education Act, which amended the law relating to school admissions, meant that this research became particularly pertinent.

Acknowledgements

The project team would like to express their gratitude to all those whose ready cooperation and assistance have enabled this research to be undertaken.

We are particularly grateful to the large number of parents in the four case study authorities who kindly completed questionnaires, and to the LEA officers, heads and teachers in those same authorities who have willingly given of their time in interviews and discussions. We would also like to thank the many LEA officers across the country who completed questionnaires.

We are indebted to our steering committee (the members of which are listed opposite) for their advice and sustained interest in the parental choice project as well as for their comments on the drafts of this report.

Within the NFER we would wish to thank Margaret I. Reid, the project director, for contributing a great deal of time and work, Joanna Le Métais and Sue Taylor for most usefully and thoroughly commenting on the penultimate draft of this report, Cres Fernandes for his assistance in the statistical analyses and last, but not least, Christine Negus, our secretary.

IPC Steering Committee

Sir Edward Britton (Chairman) – Vice-President,
NFER Board of Management

Mrs Suzanne Burn – Commission for Local
Administration

Peter Cornall – Senior County Inspector of
Schools,
Cornwall County Council

Peter Cotgrove – NFER Board of Management

Ms Veda Dovaston – NFER-Nelson Publishing
Company

Dr John Gray – University of Sheffield

Mike Williams – Department of Education
and Science

Mrs Beti Wyn Thomas – National Consumer Council

CHAPTER 1

Introduction

The issue of parental involvement in education, and more specifically in the choice of school, has been a recurring theme in educational and political discussion for many years. Proponents of the idea that parents should have a greater say in how and where their children are educated have emerged among educational practitioners and theorists and from right across the political spectrum. On the other hand, in more recent years there does not appear to have been any such organized lobby from the parents themselves. Perhaps this is not particularly surprising, since it is difficult to imagine how one body could represent the diverse views of the parent population, for whom often the only common link might be parenthood itself. Furthermore, it may be that relatively few parents have strong views about the rights or wrongs of choice, and that those who do can communicate this via local political channels to national level.

The arguments put forward in support of choice have been found to vary enormously. There appear to be five main arguments: (1) there are those who take the view that it is a fundamental right of every parent to decide upon all matters relating to their child's future; (2) others are in favour of allowing parents to choose a school which is suited to their child's needs; (3) some believe that parental involvement has a beneficial effect on a child's perceptions of and motivations towards school; (4) others argue that parental choice will improve the quality of what schools have to offer by encouraging the stimulus of competition through market forces; (5) still others argue that it will improve education as a whole by increasing accountability.

Those who are against increased parental choice also represent a variety of viewpoints: (1) some feel that the additional strain on LEA resources would amount to unjustifiable public expenditure; (2) others believe that the operation of market forces would have a disastrous effect on unpopular schools and thus would not only jeopardize the quality of education for the children therein, but also the possibility of a 'local' school for future generations of children; (3) still others do not think that the majority of parents choose schools for the right reasons and therefore parental choice may force schools to respond in a way which is harmful to their true educational and social goals. Whilst all of these views were of interest to the project team, and indeed many of them have shaped parts of our inquiry, it was not the purpose of this research to decide upon the merits or otherwise of giving parents a choice of school. The views expressed in the report about this issue have been derived directly from those LEA officers, heads or parents who were involved in the study.

The passing of the 1980 Education Act and the subsequent 1981 Department of Education and Science Regulations could be seen jointly to constitute a milestone in the continuing parental choice debate, since they strive respectively to provide parents with greater choice of school and more information to help them decide. Whilst many people felt that the Act did not appear likely to change the state of play radically, others perceived in the new procedural requirements and the phrasing of the parents' right to express a preference, a major development. Sections 6, 7 and 8 of the Act, which deal specifically with admissions to schools, are printed in full in Appendix 2.1, 2.2 and 2.3. However, it may be helpful to quote the most relevant parts here.

Section 6 (1), (2) and (3) states:

(1)   Every local education authority shall make arrangements for enabling the parent of a child in the area of the authority to express a preference as to the school at which he wishes education to be provided for his child in the exercise of the authority's functions and to give reasons for his preference.

(2)   Subject to subsection (3) below, it shall be the duty of a local education authority and of the governors of a county or voluntary school to comply with any preference expressed in accordance with the arrangements.

(3)   The duty imposed by subsection (2) above does not apply –

 (*a*) if compliance with the preference would prejudice the provision of efficient education or the efficient use of resources;

 (*b*) if the preferred school is an aided or special agreement school and compliance with the preference would be incompatible with any arrangements between the governors and the local education authority in respect of the admission of pupils to the school; or

 (*c*) if the arrangements for admission to the preferred school are based wholly or partly on selection by reference to ability or aptitude and compliance with the preference would be incompatible with selection under the arrangements.

The next chapter describes in detail the development of the parental choice debate and progression towards the 1980 Act. However, it is important to draw attention to the two main points which arise from the above quotation. First, the Act places clear limitations on the requirement of an LEA to comply with parents' wishes, thus sowing the inevitable seeds of dispute as to what constitutes efficient use of education and resources. Secondly, the Act consistently uses the term 'preference' as opposed to 'choice', thus again giving scope for misinterpretation. Whilst some may mistakenly believe the two words to be interchangeable, there is in fact a subtle, yet crucial difference between allowing parents to express a preference, and giving them an actual choice. The former is the seeking of a viewpoint, whilst the latter implies the agreement to grant whatever that viewpoint may dictate. These two points in the Act were found to be crucial, especially when LEAs were trying to interpret what the implications of the new legislation were for them.

Both the 1980 Act and 1981 DES Regulations came into official operation for transfer in autumn 1982. The Information for Parental Choice Project started one year later, and was therefore in a position to examine the procedures during their second year of use, as well as to inquire about the initial implementation and reaction to them. During the first year of the research, the project team worked in cooperation with four LEAs which were selected so that a range of current LEA procedures and school practices for providing parents with information could be studied. These LEAs provided examples of choice in four different contexts:

(a) A compact urban area with a two-tier selective system.
(b) A compact urban area with a comprehensive system.
(c) A well spaced rural area with a two-tier selective system.
(d) A well spaced rural area with a comprehensive system.

In each of these LEAs, one area (usually one town) was selected for study so that the dynamics of the local situation could be explored. Only in the compact urban comprehensive LEA did this differ. Because this LEA was a London borough with many schools, four schools were selected to highlight a range of popularity and practice.

Besides attending talks given by secondary heads, and parents' meetings in primary schools, the project team interviewed LEA officers and heads of both primary and secondary schools in order to gain an insight into the way the different LEA contexts affected the type of choice available and the range of information available. In addition, in order to ascertain how parents make their decisions, and their responses to their LEA's procedures, a sample of parents of pupils who transferred to a school other than their 'local' or catchment-area secondary school in September 1983 were interviewed.

During the second year of the research, the project team further explored some of the issues raised in previous discussions with parents through a questionnaire survey to all those parents whose children transferred in September 1984 to the 18 schools in the four case-study LEAs. In three of these four LEAs, the parents received a questionnaire after their child had transferred to the secondary school. In the fourth LEA, the London borough, the questionnaire was sent to parents after the allocation of a secondary school place, but before transfer. The reason for the different sampling procedure related to the different transfer patterns and is explained in Chapter 5. Each of the questionnaires was piloted in another area of its LEA before distribution to parents.

The parents' responses reveal a variety of interesting features – not least that their perceptions and reactions appear to be influenced by three main aspects – LEA policy, school practice and their own social and educational background. A key part of the questionnaire dealt with why parents favoured some schools more than others. When asked what aspects were important to them when choosing a school, an open-ended question format produced 7689 useful reasons which were coded into 97 categories. Thus both qualitative and quantitative information on parents' views was collected.

In the second year of the research, besides surveying the views of parents, it had originally been intended to conduct a national questionnaire survey of schools to gain an overall picture of admissions procedures. However, the first year's work indicated that whilst the activities of individual schools created a noticeable impression on parents, it was the context in which the schools operated, i.e. the LEA organization and policy, which exerted a far greater impact on the parents when they sought a secondary school for their child. Therefore, instead of a school study, it was decided to conduct a questionnaire survey of LEA admissions practice in England and Wales.

In order to gain a good response rate, this 'LEA' questionnaire was limited to only four sides of A4 paper, and the information gained was supplemented with details obtained from the LEA parents' booklet. At least one questionnaire was sent to every authority, but where practice differed between areas within an authority, each of the divisional officers was requested to complete a separate form. The authorities returned 125 completed questionnaires representing in part, or fully, 81 of the 104 LEAs in England and Wales. In addition, parents' booklets were received from 100 LEAs and from them the supplementary information was extracted. For this reason the total numbers given in tables giving detail on LEA practice (Chapters 3 and 4) will differ according to whether the information gained was derived from the LEA questionnaires (N = 125) or the LEA brochures (N = 100). As well as the questionnaire and brochure information, education officers from 45 areas or LEAs were interviewed. These were selected to represent a range of practice, taking into account such aspects as catchment areas, the number of appeals held and the percentage of these which were upheld. The information obtained revealed that local authorities differed enormously both in their educational policies and their administration of school allocations, and that the root of this variation seemed to lie in the existing variety of LEA procedures upon which the 1980 Act and 1981 Regulations were superimposed.

In presenting this report the authors have adopted a structure which first sets the historical and political context of the parental choice debate (Chapter 2), then describes the current situation regarding LEA policy and practice in admissions procedures and the publication of information (Chapters 3 and 4). The parents' responses in terms of LEA, school and social influences are described in Chapters 5 and 6. Chapter 7 describes the point at which LEA administration and parents come into direct and individual conflict – namely in appeals procedures. In the final chapter there is no attempt to make policy recommendations and no decision is reached as to the justification or otherwise of parental choice. Instead, the authors seek to highlight the fairly common discrepancies between LEA policy and practice by describing what practical procedures are required to reflect certain policies.

CHAPTER 2

The Evolving Balance Between Parents and LEAs

The Background to the 1980 Education Act

Although the 1980 Education Act has recently focused attention on to the issues of parental choice of school, the arguments have been well rehearsed in the past. J.S. Mill, for example, in his essay 'On Liberty' (1859) advocated a system of 'choice for all' which would be made possible by government support for those otherwise unable to meet the costs of education. Three-quarters of a century later, in 1926, Francis Cardinal Bourne argued that parents should be presented with an annual coupon or warrant for the cost-per-child amount. This would entitle the child to a place in any recognized school in the neighbourhood (Oldmeadow, 1944). More recently, reference to parental wishes appeared in the 1944 Education Act as a 'General Principle to be observed by Minister and local education authorities':

> In the exercise and performance of all powers and duties conferred and imposed on them by this Act the Minister and local education authorities shall have regard to the general principle that, so far as is compatible with the provision of efficient instruction and training and the avoidance of unreasonable public expenditure, pupils are to be educated in accordance with the wishes of their parents.
>
> Education Act 1944, s.76

Care, however, must be exercised in accepting any of these three statements as straightforward arguments with applicability to today's contexts. Mill was writing at a time when private education predominated: he wanted government support for education but he totally abhorred the concept of a monopolized state education. He believed that the only way to encourage diversity of opinion and individuality in the population was through diversity of education, paid for, but not run, by the state (Mill, 1859). Similarly, Cardinal Bourne's warrants were products of a very different education system. In this case, whilst he believed that the warrants would 'relieve poor parents of social disability and would vivify education by a spirit of wholesome rivalry', his main reason for advocating them was to remove the financial inequity that burdened a considerable number of tax- and rate-paying Roman Catholic and Anglican parents who chose, and paid for, confessional schools for their children (Oldmeadow, 1944). State education in 1926 was otherwise free and paid out of the taxes and rates.

In both these examples we see evidence of themes and ideas that will reappear many years later as arguments for parental choice, although they will all have been refurbished to match modern contexts. However, section 76 of the 1944 Act is in a different position since its current, popular interpretation of offering LEA adherence to parental wishes in the choice between like schools was never its original intention. In view of the regularity with which this section is quoted as laying down the principles of modern 'parental choice' it is perhaps as well to consider how it entered the statute book and what it was intended to mean.

In December 1943, R.A. Butler, the President of the Board of Education, presented to the House of Commons an Education Bill to reform the law relating to education in England and Wales. This was its First Reading. The main principles behind this Bill, and the subsequent Education Act 1944, had been published some six months earlier in a far-sighted White Paper entitled 'Educational Reconstruction' (Board of Education, 1943). It is notable that nowhere in the White Paper or the Bill are parents' wishes mentioned.

On 19th January 1944, during the Bill's Second Reading Debate, this point was taken up by Mr Magnay: 'I ask that those who want religious education should not be denied it' (H.C. Deb., Vol. 396, Col. 301). Similarly, in the next speech, Mr Ivor Thomas, in seeking the abolition of the 'dual system', required the guarantee: 'that all children whose parents so desire shall be brought up in the faith of their parents' (H.C. Deb., Vol. 396, Col. 305). Mr Butler conceded this point on the next day and commented that in view of the government's intention, 'to bring parents in more than we have done before', they would look into this issue during the later stages of the Bill (H.C. Deb., Vol. 396, Col. 428: 20th Jan. 1944).

On 20th June that year, in the House of Lords, the duty to accede to parents' wishes wherever possible was introduced as a new paragraph into the Bill. It was listed as clause 8(2)(b), as clause 8 dealt with general duties the LEAs were supposed to fulfil. Although it was not phrased in denominational terms, the Earl of Selborne's comment that failure to fulfil this duty would be a 'form of religious intolerance' makes the context very clear (H.L. Committee, Vol. 132, Col. 287: 20th June 1944).

Three weeks later, on 11th July 1944, this duty to parents was taken out of clause 8 and on the next day inserted as a 'General Principle' to follow clause 73 (H.L. Deb., Vol. 132, Col. 864). Allowing for slight renumbering this is the first time it appears in the form we know it today. Whilst the change of place in the Bill was to give the clause an applicability across all parts of the Bill, and not just to those types of school named in clause 8, there was no reference to any broadening of its scope in other respects. With the passing of the 1944 Act this clause became section 76 (as given on page 7) and explicitly laid the principles for parental choice of school. However, it implicitly only referred to a denominational choice: in the context of what was being discussed at the time the insertion of a denominational rider would have seemed superfluous.

Since then section 76 has been given a much wider interpretation and it is interesting that speaking in an education debate in the House of Lords in 1974, Lord Butler, the 'architect' of the 1944 Act, commented that in respect to affording parents their wishes (of like schools) section 76 went 'as far as any legislation can go'. He also confirmed that the common interpretation of the section was in fact mistaken:

> The origin of Section 76 was rather different from what some people imagine . . . The object of that settlement and of Section 76 was to give Roman Catholic and Anglican parents a choice of school.
>
> H.L. Deb., Vol. 353, Col. 590: 10th July 1974

For all the rights and wrongs of the wider interpretation of section 76, it has had a very marked impact on current education legislation. However, the growth of the parents' case over the last 40 years has been no smooth passage. As the social, economic and political climates changed, so the balance of the arguments between parents and LEAs swayed back and forth, but overall there was a slow but recognizable move towards the parents. The Education Act of 1980 may perhaps best be perceived as an attempt to reinforce and legitimize one position in this changing balance, a balance that had been evolving ever since 1944.

Arising out of this, any study of the implementation of the 1980 Act is virtually bound to consider the forces which bear upon the balance between the parents and LEAs. To do this it is necessary to trace the Act's development and to identify the themes which have become associated with it and which have influenced the course of its evolution. Fortunately for the research, because of their involvement, these themes also offer an appropriate framework with which to structure the inquiry into the current implementation.

In the immediate post-1944 days the issue of parental wishes in school allocation aroused little concern except that a number of admissions appeals and complaints were going to the Minister based upon sections 37 and 68 of the 1944 Act. Complaints under both these headings mainly centred around the interpretation of the word 'unreasonable' though in slightly different contexts. Section 37(2) set up School Attendance Orders and these allowed the parent to select the school to be attended, and only that school would be named in the Order unless the Minister directed otherwise. Section 37(3) allowed the LEA to ask the Minister for a direction if the LEA thought the parents had selected an 'unsuitable' or 'unreasonable' school – unreasonable that is, on the grounds of expense, and section 37(4) allowed the parents to ask the Minister for a direction if the LEA had rejected the parents' choice: again the LEA's only grounds being those of unreasonableness or inexpediency. Section 68 was wider in scope and simply considered whether an LEA had acted or proposed to act unreasonably in the exercise of its powers and duties. As there was a General Principle regarding the education of pupils in accordance with the parents' wishes (section 76) parents could use section 68 to argue that the LEA was acting unreasonably in its duty to comply with section 76 if it failed to give them the school of their choice.

As a consequence of the debatable nature of these appeals, in 1946, the Ministry of Education issued Circular 83, 'Choice of

Schools', in order to clarify the issues surrounding parents' and LEAs' 'rights' without actually committing the Minister to anything very specific in case she (Ellen Wilkinson – Labour) had to pronounce on an appeal. The aim does not seem to have been to alter the amount of 'parental choice' so much as to let the authorities know the guidelines that would be used by the Minister in those cases where the parents' choice might be argued to involve the LEA in extra expenditure. Effectively it was hoped that these guidelines would reduce the mismatch between the authority and ministry, and thus also reduce the administrative work and the number of central appeals (i.e. appeals that are dealt with by central government as opposed to local government).

It is apparent that choice between like schools, i.e. schools of a similar organization, type or status, had yet to be fully accepted. In Circular 83 the Minister was still basically concerned with choice based on selection, denomination, or ease of access. Only as a last alternative did she mention a fourth, possible and somewhat ambiguous, reason for choice: 'Educational considerations, e.g. the provision of a particular type of advanced work in an individual school.' This implicit assumption in Circular 83 that choice between like schools was of little importance was even more evident when the Minister commented on primary schools:

> In the case of primary education the question of selecting a school of a particular educational type does not arise . . . parents generally may be expected to select the school of the appropriate age range most convenient to their homes.
>
> Ministry of Education, 1946

Four years later, on 23rd August 1950, the Ministry of Education, under the Labour government, published its 'Manual of Guidance: Schools No. 1', again entitled 'Choice of Schools'. Once more the main reason for publication was to allow LEAs to understand how the Minister was dealing with appeals, and in this respect it may be seen as an expanded form of its 1946 predecessor. However, for the first time a government document really opened up the range of what might be chosen. Thus, whilst it commenced with a qualification: 'At the onset it should be noted that Section 76 does not confer on the parent complete freedom of choice', on the very next page it stated: 'Section 76 is not limited to choices made on denominational grounds. Nor does it apply merely to the initial choice of a school'. The leaflet offered three 'strong' reasons for parents choosing an alternative school: (1) denominational; (2) educational (provision of a particular type of advanced work in a particular school); (3) the linguistic character of the school (i.e. Welsh or English medium). A further five reasons which an LEA could 'properly take account of' were also given: (4) convenience of access; (5) the existence of special facilities at a school (e.g. provision of mid-day meals thus allowing parents to work all day); (6) preference for a single sex or mixed school; (7) family association with a particular school; (8) medical reasons.

Whilst increasing the number of acceptable reasons in 1950 the Minister also saw fit to strengthen the administrative argument against choice. Here we see one of the first overt references to the idea of it being a 'balance':

> The practical problem of administration, therefore, which faces local education authorities is how far effect should be given to the parents' wishes . . . Some of the relevant considerations (i.e. the strengths of the parents' and LEA's arguments) . . . may need to be balanced against each other before a decision is reached.
>
> Ministry of Education, 1950

The reasons for refusing parental choice were given as follows: (a) overcrowding and 'zoning'; (b) attendance at all-age, un-reorganized schools; (c) the avoidance of unreasonable public expenditure; (d) extra-district charges; (e) transport costs and time of journey. All but 'all-age schools' and the issue of 'extra-district charges' are still in use in 1986. (See Chapter 3.)

Compared with the post-1980 position this balance of relevant considerations favoured LEAs far more than parents, and in the 20 years between the early 1950s and 1970s it changed little. However, in other aspects of education there were major upheavals of which the most significant was the introduction of comprehensive schooling, a development which had surprising ramifications for parental choice.

In 1951, having lost the general election, the Labour Party reshaped some of its policies and one idea that had been in the movement for some time, the belief in comprehensive education, was brought out as a major policy (Middleton and Weitzman, 1976). However, from 1951 to 1964 a pro-selective, Conservative government was in office and for the most part selective schooling ruled the day. With the return of the Labour government in the 1964 election, the comprehensive ideal was emphasized and reorganization set in motion with Circular 10/65 (DES, July 1965). However, both the necessary supporting legislation, and the Green Paper which fully expounded Labour's policies, failed to see the light of day before the Conservatives regained office in 1970. Amongst other proposals in Edward Short's 1970 unpublished Green Paper were plans for stronger rights for parents, independent appeals, easier transfers and parental participation on governing bodies (*The Times*, 25th March 1969). The ideas were not totally lost, however, as some of them reappeared two years later, somewhat abridged, in *Labour's Programme for Britain* (Labour Party, 1972).

With the Black Papers firmly supporting them, the Conservative government of 1970–1974 maintained an anti-comprehensive stance in public but recognized that not all conservative councils shared this view. The then government's enthusiasm for paying regard to the wishes of parents could be seen as having three parts: (a) the parents' choice of type of state school system for their locality and thus, implicitly, for their child; (b) the parents' choice between the independent or state sectors; and (c) lastly, and somewhat masked, the parents' choice between like, state schools. The February 1974 Conservative Manifesto demonstrates this well:

> In secondary education we shall continue to judge local education authorities' proposals for changing the character of schools on their merits, paying special regard to the wishes of parents and the retention of parental choice. We believe it to be educationally unwise to impose a universal system of comprehensive education on the entire country. Local education authorities should allow genuine scope for parental choice, and we shall continue to use our powers to give as much choice as possible.
>
> We will defend the fundamental right of parents to spend their money on their children's education should they wish to do so.

We shall continue to support the direct grant schools. They have helped to provide increased opportunities for able children irrespective of their parents' means.

We shall maintain the right of parents to choose denominational education for their children if they so wish.

Conservative Party, 1974A

In February 1974 the Conservatives lost the election and soon after, in October, were faced with another. The change in education policy between these two elections was considerable, with the attack on comprehensive education being toned down and in its place parental choice was brought forward as 'A Charter of Parents' Rights'. The recognition that being anti-comprehensive was not a substantial attraction to the electorate had encouraged an appeal to parents' 'rights' which was based, in part, upon the view that comprehensive education represented a possible denial of these 'rights'. The Conservative Party Manifesto for October 1974 explains this new parents' charter:

A Charter of Parents' Rights
An important part of the distinct Conservative policy on education is to recognise parental rights. A say in how their children are to be brought up is an essential ingredient in the parental role. We will therefore introduce additional rights for parents. First, by amending the 1944 Education Act, we will impose clear obligations on the state and local authorities to take account of the wishes of parents. Second, we will consider establishing a local appeal system for parents dissatisfied with the allotment of schools. Third, parents will be given the right to be represented on school boards – by requiring a substantial proportion of the school governors and managers to be drawn from and elected by, the parents of children currently at school. Fourth, we will place an obligation on all head teachers to form a parent-teachers association to assist and support teachers. Fifth, we will encourage schools to publish prospectuses about their record, existing character, specialities and objectives.

Conservative Party, 1974B

Of course, manifesto statements cannot be viewed in total isolation.

Parental participation fitted into a broader policy that was being proposed at the time, a policy which offered more say for young people, increased power for the Welsh Office, a Scottish Assembly, increased home-ownership and greater employee participation. Equally, the charter can be argued to have developed out of earlier ideas, some of which were very similar to those in Labour's unpublished 1970 Green Paper (Middleton and Weitzman, 1976).

The expression of parental 'choice' or even 'power' in educational decision making from then on appeared regularly in parliamentary debates. On 27th November 1974, just a month after the election, Mr William Shelton (Conservative) presented the Education (Parents' Charter) Bill for its First Reading, and speeches in its Second Reading Debate amplify many points and demonstrate how the ideas were developing. For instance, Mr Shelton suggested that one purpose of the Bill was to 'tilt the balance slightly towards parental rights, and perhaps slightly away from the local education authorities' (H.C. Deb., Vol. 890, Col. 1950: 25th April 1975). In maintaining the idea of the balance he advocated the setting up of local appeal committees as extensions of LEAs, an idea which was taken up four years later by Labour in Shirley Williams' 1978 Bill. However, protests at the time of his Bill caused him to switch to supporting the idea of an independent appeals tribunal.

Two further important themes emerged from that debate. Dr Hampson took up the issue of the necessary diversity of provision if choice was to be real, and Norman St John Stevas, as well as succinctly summarizing the potential effects of the Bill, considered the necessary order for presenting the parent and LEA arguments in the appeals and reached the conclusion that the onus was on the LEA to establish prejudice and therefore the LEA had to present its case first. In effect he anticipated this important part of the 1984 'South Glamorgan' High Court Judgement by some nine years.

The amendment proposed by my Hon. Friend is intended to make that general principle [section 76] an effective principle of action by shifting the burden of proof away from the parents, who have to prove something positively about their wishes, to saying that that is no longer necessary and that the norm now is that children should be educated in accordance with the wishes of the parents unless it can be shown positively that it is

unreasonable to do so on the ground of the cost involved. This is
an important change.

H.C. Deb., Vol. 840, Col. 1967: 25th April 1975

The Education (Parents' Charter) Bill

The Parents' Charter Bill, as a Private Members' Bill, was talked
out of the Commons and never became law in itself though many of
its features eventually reached the statute books in the 1980 Act.

At about this time though, 1974/75, vouchers were attracting a
good deal of attention. Dr Rhodes Boyson (1970) had argued most
forcibly against Edward Short's second and unpublished
Education Bill of 1970 on the grounds that it promoted
neighbourhood schools at the expense of choice and equality.
Furthermore, he had felt that the 'small' moves towards parent-
teacher associations, academic boards and so forth, that were
advocated both in the Bill and in the unpublished Green Paper,
would not be sufficient to meet the ever-increasing 'demand' for
parental choice. His answer to this 'demand' was an extension of
fee-paying education (private or state) supported by vouchers – a
system which 'would transform the educational scene' with the
transformation resulting from the improved diversity of provision
(but only where the various types of school were successful in
attracting parental support), and from the increased parental
involvement in education (*ibid.*). The degree of parental
involvement is interesting and was taken up later by William
Shelton when he suggested that the Parents' Charter would only
'involve marginally another 10 per cent of parents in the education
of their children' (H.C. Deb., Vol. 890, Col. 1967: 25th April 1975).

On the Labour side vouchers were regarded with abhorrence.
The Parliamentary Under-Secretary for Education, Mr Armstrong,
replying on behalf of the Secretary of State to a parliamentary
question in May 1975, said that the Secretary of State was on record
as seeing 'no merit in, and serious objections to, the voucher
system'. On a point about whether the voucher system could restore
parental choice Mr Armstrong replied:

> We have to face reality, which is that up to 85 per cent of our
> children will have no choice at all. The voucher system is seen by
> the Government as being socially devisive. On principle we are

against it . . . Education is not to be sold across the counter like groceries. It is far more important.

H.C. Oral Questions, Vol. 891, Col. 1202: 6th May 1975

For all the (Labour) government's concern, Kent County Council commissioned a feasibility study in 1975 to look into the viability of translating the voucher theory into practice (Kent County Council, 1978). Having finally rejected vouchers as being impractical they later attempted an experiment with a somewhat diluted form known as 'open enrolment'. The outcome of this experiment, which is now history in itself, was that to follow even this approach was too expensive within a state system. For whatever reasons, the Kent parents were not of a single mind such that all schools could be equally full, or even mostly full, with the rest being completely emptied. In practice some schools needed extra classrooms whilst others, with reduced intakes, still had to be kept open to satisfy a diminished but still significant, local demand. It is difficult to imagine a more expensive way of managing schools. (*The Guardian*, 12th August 1983, 'Schools Choice Scheme Hits Trouble'.)

In 1976 the minority Labour government presented an Education Bill to hasten comprehensive reorganization, but the compulsory elements in the Bill seriously antagonized the Conservative opposition. Due to the vagueness of its full title, 'A Bill to Amend the Law Relating to Education', the opposition was free to insert extra clauses and schedules for debate – indeed the original ten clauses and no schedules became 122 clauses and nine schedules and the committee stages took 80 hours. During this debate the 'parental choice' issues were given a considerable airing. The belief that going comprehensive had reduced parental choice was put forward by Sir George Sinclair (H.C. Deb., Vol. 914, Col. 430: 30th June 1976), and the idea of how appeals boards would contribute to the goal in Conservative policy 'that the right to educate children belongs to the parents and not to the state' was argued by St John Stevas (H.C. Deb., Vol. 914, Col. 461: 30th June 1976).

Up to 1976 most parental allocation complaints and appeals to the Secretary of State had been based upon section 68 of the 1944 Act, and only relatively few complaints had been based upon section 37(3) with School Attendance Orders. As described earlier, both sections required the Secretary of State to interpret the word 'reasonable', although only the latter, section 37, required the child to be kept out of school for the Secretary of State to become involved. A Draft Circular to LEAs in 1976 entitled 'Admission of Children to Schools of their Parents' Choice' claimed that the arguments for the two clauses were sufficiently similar such that:

> He (the Secretary of State) normally decides choice of school complaints under Section 68 on the same criteria as those prescribed in Section 37(3) . . . There is therefore, in principle, no advantage to a parent in keeping his child from school.
>
> DES, 1976

The 'Tameside judgement' in 1976 offered a new interpretation which effectively meant that the Secretary of State could no longer be satisfied under section 68 that an authority was acting or proposing to act unreasonably unless no reasonable authority could ever act in that way (see Fowler, 1979, and Bull, 1986). Since 1976 there have been very few instances of a Secretary of State giving directions to an LEA concerning allocations under section 68 (Bull, 1985). However, section 37 was unaffected by this judgement, and arguably because of this, and more certainly because it required the LEA to defend its position rather than the parents having to defend their case, it is claimed that this section became a more powerful approach for parents to take (Fowler, 1979).

Over the years the number of central appeals had grown dramatically. Prior to comprehensive reorganization the combined number of appeals to the Secretary of State had approached about 100 per year. After reorganization and into the 1970s this number climbed to around 1000 or more per year – a tenfold increase (DES, 1977B). Even though the parents' success rate was very thin – for example in 1977 only two out of 1124 section 68 complaints and only 24 out of 40 section 37 appeals were upheld (Passmore, 1983; Meredith, 1981; Newell, 1983) – this large number of appeals was becoming a problem in itself.

Furthermore, the political climate in the 1970s was such that it can be argued that appeals were beginning to be taken much more seriously. This large number of central appeals consequently presented an embarrassment to both the DES and the LEAs and the fact that children were being kept out of school so as to bring about section 37 appeals was further thought to be educationally most unsatisfactory (DES, 1977B; Bennett, H.C. Deb. Education

(No. 2) Bill, Standing Committee D, Col. 619, 1979). Something had to be done.

There were in 1976/77 three recognizable pressures on the Labour government: (1) a perceived growing demand for parental choice; (2) imminent falling rolls; and (3) an embarrassing problem of appeals. The 1977 Consultation Paper, 'Admission of Children to Schools of their Parents' Choice', presented Shirley Williams' potential solutions to all three points. Amongst other things it suggested that:

(1)   Parental preference should be regarded as having a degree of intrinsic validity and must be given a channel of expression that allows it to be taken into account together with other factors from the outset of the allocation procedure.

(2)   LEAs should be able to plan the operating capacity of their schools and to refuse a child a place at a particular school (unless there are special reasons to the contrary) if the school is full to that capacity.

(3)   Each authority's arrangements should also include a procedure for local appeals. Normally (i.e. when this operated) the Secretary of State would not consider a complaint from a parent until the case had been considered on appeal. Section 37(3) of the 1944 Act would be repealed and consequential amendments made to section 37(4). Questions of admissions to schools would be specifically excluded from consideration under section 68.

DES, 1977B

(N.b. Local appeals at this stage were not necessarily to be run under the auspices of the Council on Tribunals.)

Whilst these proposals may be described as moving the balance towards the parent (Shirley Williams, 1985), others may see it differently since the arguments emphasizing the LEAs' management role and allowing them to block choice were once again strengthened. Thus although it was proposed that it would become a statutory requirement to accede to the parents' wishes, the clauses allowing exceptions to be made would now include:

(a)   breaching the planned operating capacity as determined by the LEA;

(b)   adverse affects to the efficient provision of education in the school *or* in the area, *or* being in conflict with the comprehensive principle as described in section 1 of the Education Act 1976; and

(c)   if the school was unsuitable to the age, ability or aptitude of the child.

The parents' final redress to an appeal was also to be potentially weakened. The Labour Secretary of State was proposing that 'appeals' should be LEA reviews of LEA decisions and that she should only be brought in on procedural matters, i.e. appeals under section 37(3) and 37(4) were to be routed back to the LEA instead of the Minister and the right to appeal under section 68 for allocation decisions was to be removed. Thus Labour's 1977 response to the Parents' Charter was, in essence, a management charter. LEAs were to be given more strength to handle falling rolls and central allocation appeals were to be phased out.

For the most part, these 1977 recommendations appeared in similar form one year later in the 1978 Education Bill, but there was one small but significant change that further shifted the balance towards the LEAs. In Labour's 1976 draft Green Paper it stated that 'the Secretary of State hopes that authorities will be flexible about admissions from other areas of adjoining authorities to fill marginal places'. A year later the Secretary of State was stated as believing, 'that there should, as far as possible, be "free trade" across local authority boundaries' (DES, 1977B). But by 1978 the Secretary of State was intent on repealing that part of the London Government Act of 1963 which prevented LEAs in Greater London refusing admission on the grounds that the pupil lived in another London borough (see Chapter 4, page 52). If 'choice' and falling rolls were to be managed, then it seems that cross-boundary transfers with equal rights were not to be encouraged in the Greater London area at least.

The 1980 Education Act

The 1978 Bill failed to reach the statute books as the Labour government went to the polls too soon for its progress through Parliament to be completed. The new Conservative government brought in two Education Acts in quick succession. The first, in 1979, simply served to overturn the 1976 Education Act and to remove the element of compulsory comprehensive reorganization. The second, the 1980 Education Act, with many elements of the old Labour 1978 Bill, shifted the balance once more towards the parents in line with the current Conservative philosophy. (See Appendices 2.1 to 2.3 for sections 6, 7 and 8 of the Education Act 1980.) That the Act is so similar to the 1978 Bill is really not surprising since the three major problems the 1978 Bill set out to alleviate were still present: i.e. (1) the perceived demand for parental choice; (2) falling rolls, and (3) an embarrassing number of appeals to the Secretary of State.

In moving the balance back towards the parents the question of how far it could go was seriously contended within the party. For example, it was asked whether there was any need for admissions limits. Could not the system operate perfectly well on market forces alone? If there needed to be a curb, could it not be solely based upon the efficient provision and cost of resources argument? In the end Mark Carlisle (Conservative Secretary of State for Education) upheld the use of a guide figure, in this case the '*intended* intake', but he gave it no force of law in its own right: he simply required it to be published for parents' information. However, the Act permitted three reasons for an LEA not to comply with parental preference: (a) if compliance with the preference would prejudice the provision of efficient education or the efficient use of resources; (b) if compliance would clash with the principles of a voluntary-aided or special agreement school: or (c) if compliance would clash with selective principles. (For the full version of section 6(3) of the 1980 Act see Appendix 2.1.) In Circular 1/81 the DES suggests that the intended intake figure should 'be the number beyond which the authority or governors would normally refuse to make further admissions to the school' (DES, 1981A). Thus, if the LEA ties the intended intake to reason (a) above, then the figure effectively becomes the maximum intake for efficiency (so to speak) and can therefore ride with the legal status of the efficient education and resources argument.

One of the features of the 1980 Act is that it recognized and allowed for an amount of LEA autonomy and thus the problems of defining 'efficient education or the efficient use of resources' could not readily be centrally resolved. As it was not wished to give LEAs unlimited power to decide that parental rights could be overrun (Boyson, H.C. Deb., Standing Ctte. D: 4th Dec. 1979), it was felt that some form of local appeal should be instigated to maintain the balance between the parents' and the LEA's rights, and in the voluntary-aided sector, between the parents' and the school governors' 'rights'. The local authorities were offered either (a) an appeal committee with an LEA majority, the decision of which would be binding, or (b) a committee with no such majority, whose decision would be advisory only. The local authority associations were in no doubt that the former alternative was the right solution (Bull, 1980).

The appeal committees were intended to carry out two functions: first, they could decide between individual parents and the LEA or voluntary-aided school governors, and secondly, because the LEA or the voluntary-aided school governors would be responsive to their decisions, the committees could influence the allocation decisions in the first place. (Boyson, H.C. Deb., Education (No. 2) Bill, Standing Committee D., Cols. 553 and 542 respectively: 11th Dec. 1979.)

Having presented this powerful pro-parent role for the appeal committees, Dr Boyson further suggested that they would be unlikely to turn down appeals for schools where the LEA had recently reduced the number of places and left spare capacity available (Boyson, *ibid.*, Col. 553). To achieve this the appeal committees might be thought of as being independent, but this was clearly not what was intended. In the same debate Dr Boyson argued that:

> There is a majority of members appointed by the local education authority to make sure that the policy of that authority as implemented in the way in which children are allocated to schools can be checked up on there and then. I would find it very odd if a majority representation of the local education authority on the appeal tribunal were to create a vast problem for itself by putting 200 more children into a school where there was no room

for them. I should imagine that the local education authority would have something to say to its nominees about that.

> Boyson, *ibid.*, Col. 552

Dr Boyson returned to this theme a little later:

> I cannot see that there would be any conflict between a local authority and its own appeal tribunal. It would be a funny local authority which set up all kinds of appeal tribunals which were in constant battle with the local authority.
>
> Boyson, *ibid.*, Col. 630

And the same argument was again offered a little later still:

> Local education authorities will, after all, have a majority of members on appeal committees, and that ought to be sufficient to safeguard their legitimate interests.
>
> Neil MacFarlane, *ibid.*, Col. 738

Clearly, the national legislation has attempted to move the balance towards the parents but the final decision lies with the appeal committees which appear to have been asked to play contradictory roles. Their pro-parent role must be set against their composition which gives them a majority of LEA or voluntary-aided school appointees. Further, as the appeal committees must take the LEAs' or schools' published admissions arrangements into account, we can see the parent and LEA or parent and school balance being not only localized, but once more, LEA or school influenced. For all these factors it would still appear that, on the whole, the balance was meant to shift towards the parents. What is not certain is either how far it shifted or how stable it is given that the parent/LEA relationship is evolving rapidly through the changing influence of the appeals.

There are of course many other features of the 1980 Act which must be taken into account by any research project studying its implementation. For the most part these features are peripheral to the main 'balance' argument but significant in terms of local authority cost or work, and indeed in terms of the political debate. The five most important of these features are listed overleaf.

(1)   The provision of information for parents has accompanied all the proposals since 1974. By 1979/80 this requirement had become very specific with a detailed list of minimum topics to be included. See Schedules 1 and 2 to DES Statutory Instrument 630 (DES, 1981C).

(2)   For a Conservative government parental choice is enhanced by the assisted places scheme whereby in a limited number of instances, help can be given with the fees to independent schools (section 17 of the 1980 Act). By 1984/85 the number of 'assisted pupils' had risen to 17,336, which represents an estimated 0.25 per cent of the maintained school population. (Source: *Education*, 'Parliament', 12th July 1985.)

(3)   It was noted that the Labour government's thinking changed from 1976 to 1978 with regard to the encouragement it should give to cross-boundary transfers. The 1980 Act is in no doubt about this. Thus the duty of an LEA to comply with parents' wishes also applies to 'any application for the admission to a school maintained by a local education authority of a child who is not in the area of the authority' (section 6(5) (*a*) of the 1980 Act: Appendix 2.1). In the same vein, section 31(8) (*a*) of the 1963 London Government Act was not repealed in the 1980 Act and thus it is difficult to stop cross-boundary transfers in London (see page 52). This has, however, led to some problems and it is now understood that this part of the London Government Act will be excluded from the 1986 Act in the near future.

(4)   Both the 1978 Bill and the 1980 Act set out to reduce central appeals on matters of allocation. The 1980 Act has re-routed section 37 appeals back to the local appeal committee and therefore removed the point of keeping children out of school. However, section 68 was not repealed. In 1982 there were approximately 300 complaints to the Secretary of State under this section, and, although none of them was upheld, the problem has not completely gone away (Newell, 1983).

(5)   The role of the Secretary of State for Education with regard to local decisions is still potentially significant particularly in respect of the availability of places. Parental choice is obviously influenced by the availability and location of places, but spare places are difficult to justify economically and in any case, LEAs are required to remove a proportion of their surplus places under Circular 2/81: DES, 1981B. In the efficient management of their schools at a time

of falling rolls some authorities might wish to maintain viable school sizes by closing whole schools and redistributing future pupils, whilst others might prefer to reduce all their schools by a set proportion. Either way, if an authority wishes to reduce a school's size by 20 per cent or more, or if it wishes to change its character significantly, or to close it, the LEA is liable to incur the Secretary of State's intervention (sections 13 and 15, 1980 Act). If, in reaching a judgement, the Secretary of State uses criteria which are alien to those in use by the LEA then he will have an impact on the balance which is potentially neither consonant with the policies of the locally elected politicians, nor with the practice of the local appeals committee.

Conclusion

The 1980 Act came into force on 1st October 1980 and applied for the first time to admissions to school in the autumn of 1982. As it came into operation the Manual of Guidance (Schools No. 1), entitled 'Choice of Schools' was formally withdrawn – a rather apposite move since it was in this 1950 document that parental 'choice' of like schools first really received ministerial attention (Ministry of Education, 1950). As has been described the main reasons for the Act relate to (a) a perceived growing demand for parental choice, (b) falling rolls, and (c) the need to rectify a very unsatisfactory central appeals situation. As with the 1978 Education Bill the Act has strong management overtones. But there have also been claims that through its emphasis on choice the Act would bring about improved parental involvement (St John Stevas, 1977; Atherton, 1979) and indeed, better schooling (Sugarman, 1979, Joseph, 1982). The Education Act 1980 can thus be seen to have been introduced to meet political, management and educational aims, with the crux of any changes depending on the balance between parents and LEAs shifting in the parents' favour. The question as to whether any movement of this balance is good or bad is beyond the remit of this research. What the research can do, however, is to illuminate the processes and arguments involved and aim to offer a clearer understanding of what is being done.

CHAPTER 3

LEA Administration of Secondary School Admissions

The previous chapter, which described the legislative background to the 1980 Act, has indicated the context for this investigation of the processes involved in parental choice. However, from an early stage in this research it was apparent that the nature of the choice offered depended as much on the varying local authority policies and practices as on government legislation. This impression was gained initially from the project's involvement with the four case-study authorities and was subsequently reinforced by the questionnaire and interview responses from either whole LEAs or distinct areas within LEAs[1], and from the LEA brochures. In many of the interviews an LEA officer would assume that some aspect of the procedure which his or her authority was operating was not only the obvious approach, but also common practice. In fact the project team found great diversity in how the different areas allowed parents to express a preference. This chapter will highlight these variations as well as some of the notable similarities in order to provide an overall impression of current admissions policies and procedures in England and Wales.

Authorities Using Catchment Areas

One of the main features in an LEA's organization of transfer procedures is the existence, or absence, of catchment areas. Some

[1] The LEA questionnaire was answered at either LEA or divisional level. Unless otherwise stated all responses will be treated equally and referred to as areas. Analysis of the make-up of these areas is available upon request. See Appendix 3.1.

authorities seemed to believe that they did not have catchment
areas, yet were clearly operating such a system, whilst others which
claimed to be working on a catchment-area basis were in fact
operating a 'free choice' system. Often these apparent
contradictions were simply due to differences in interpretation. For
the purpose of this report, therefore, an authority was considered to
be operating a catchment-area system if most parents were initially
offered a place at just one local school.

Having been offered this definition, 76 of the 125 areas (61 per
cent) reported that they were operating catchment-area systems
and 49 (39 per cent) indicated that they were not. When these areas
were classified as urban, rural or urban/rural mixed (N=59, 44 and
22 respectively), over 83 per cent of the rural areas had a catchment-
area system, compared with just over 47 per cent of urban areas and
45 per cent of urban/rural areas. That so many rural areas were
using a catchment-area system was to be expected, given the very
real constraints of both organizing and paying for transport.
However, what is perhaps surprising is the relatively high
proportion of the urban areas which were also using a catchment
system, where distance was less likely to be a constraint and where
several schools were probably within range (see Table 3.1).

Table 3.1:   Distribution of catchment-area systems by type of area

	Urban		Rural		Urban/ Rural		Total	
	N	%	N	%	N	%	N	%
With catchment areas	28	47	38	83	10	45	76	61
Without catchment areas	31	53	6	17	12	55	49	39
Total	59	100%	44	100%	22	100%	125	100%

From the interviews with LEA officers, it appeared that those
authorities which were primarily using catchment areas did so for
one or more of the following reasons:

(a)   a widely-spread, rural population made the time and cost of travel to anything but the nearest school both prohibitively expensive and tiring for pupils;

(b)   to protect staffing and curriculum (and therefore pupils) in less popular schools by balancing catchment-area figures;

(c)   to promote community-based education;

(d)   to ensure a social mix which might not otherwise occur if parents were encouraged to choose for themselves;

(e)   to promote pastoral and curricular continuity by linking primary, junior or middle schools to one secondary school;

(f)   to facilitate administration, forward planning and the accurate forecasting of numbers (though often officers reported that the reason they found catchment areas easy to administer was because they were used to operating in this way); and

(g)   because the authority 'traditionally' used this system and either had not considered changing it, or had considered it but had seen no reason to do so.

The variety of reasons given above indicates that catchment-area authorities are not a homogeneous group, in that they have varying policies which have led to the use of catchment areas. This is also indicated in their differing administration of the allocations procedure. For example, 62 per cent (47) of those areas using catchment areas did not require parents to respond to their offer of a place unless the parents wished to express a preference for an alternative school. Several officers said that the reason for this was simply to avoid superfluous paperwork in the form of parental acceptance letters since usually they would amount to 80 to 90 per cent of the transfer group. Other officers commented that it would be difficult to get every parent to respond. Some, however, pointed out that this method helped to discourage parents from expressing a preference for a school other than their catchment-area school, since to do so they would have to initiate that request.

On the other hand, the 39 per cent of those areas which required acknowledgement from all parents put forward several arguments for this procedure. First, a number of officers felt that by seeking a response from every parent they avoided receiving large numbers of late applications and complaints or excuses from parents that they had not received the official allocation notice. Secondly, some officers commented that receiving a reply from every parent actually eased the administrative process in that it enabled exact numbers to be ascertained early enough to plan staffing and to allocate any spare places with confidence. Thirdly, some authorities felt that a note from parents accepting the catchment-area school was a way of establishing a type of 'contract' with the parent, and also that it evoked a positive statement from the parent about their child going to a particular school.

Without exception, authorities which required a response from every parent sent some kind of proforma on which a reply should be made. However those authorities which only required a response from parents if they did *not* want the catchment-area school, used various procedures. Some sent an offer of a catchment-area school accompanied by a proforma on which the parents could opt for another school. Others offered to send such a proforma upon request, or told parents that they could get one from the county hall or from their child's primary school. Thirdly, some areas required parents who did not want the catchment area school to write a letter of application, stating their reasons, to the divisional or chief education officer – probably a serious hurdle to some parents. Whilst these methods do not, in themselves, alter the amount of choice available, they may discourage parents from opting out of their catchment area. Although some education officers were apparently unaware of this aspect, others acknowledged that it was one of the main purposes of operating in this way.

Other variations in LEA catchment-area policies were found in the phrasing of, and limitations on, the offer of a place. Some authorities demonstrated their commitment to catchment areas by their promise always to provide a place at the catchment-area school for any pupil living in the appropriate area, regardless of whether or not the parent chose to apply for an alternative school. Some also promised this regardless of how late the child moved into the catchment area. In contrast, other authorities informed parents that the offer of 'a reserved place' would be immediately withdrawn should the parents state a preference for an alternative school, and also pointed out that there was no guarantee that a place would still be available in the catchment-area school in the event of the preferred school being full. An example of this can be seen in the following extract from one authority's booklet:

> It must be emphasised that, where parents choose as their first preference a school other than the appropriate school for their address, and this application is unsuccessful, they may also be unsuccessful later in obtaining a place at the appropriate school if the latter is over-subscribed by applicants who have named it as their first choice.

Whilst it is desirable to inform parents of their rights, this system must surely reduce the number of parents who might otherwise express a preference for an alternative school. Also, the use of the words 'appropriate school' is interesting.

Authorities Without Catchment Areas

Authorities without catchment areas accounted for 39 per cent (49) of the questionnaire returns. In these areas it was common practice to write to parents offering several schools to choose from, either by listing them on a form, or by referring parents to the list of schools in the LEA booklet. Some authorities required parents to name only one first preference, whilst others permitted the naming of more than one school on the understanding that each school named by the parent would be treated by the admissions office as equal first preferences. If any of the schools the parents had named were subsequently offered, this would constitute an offer of a first preference, and the LEA claimed that they could not appeal against the offer of a place. Curiously, although this system appears to be radically different to the single 'first choice' approach it is in fact very similar. There are two main reasons for this. First, parents do not list many equal first choices; the 2958 parents in the 1984 transfer cohort in one LEA where this system is operated only named an average of 1.25 schools each, with 2355 of those parents putting only one school. Secondly, the processes of first and second round allocations apply here just as in the conventional system, and similarly therefore second and subsequent choices have the same reduced status.

Other 'free choice' areas asked parents to name several schools, usually two or three, and to place them in rank order. Several officers who used this system commented that it was not uncommon for a parent to name one school twice, or even three times, presumably in the hope of increasing their chances of getting their preferred school. However when this occurred and the first preference could not be met, the officer either wrote back asking the parent to name an alternative school, or more commonly, made an offer of an alternative school which still had some places available.

Most authorities said it was extremely rare, if not unknown, to be unable to offer a parent one of their initial choices. However, in one authority, if none of the three preferences could be offered to a parent, a second list was circulated which contained only the names of schools with places still available. This might be seen as restricting the range of choice, since parents may have wished to opt for schools not on the second list even though they had not asked for these schools in the first round and the authority now regarded them as full. This view must of course be tempered by some recognition of reality: it hardly seems sensible to offer schools which are 'full', and yet to restrict the parents' right to name any school goes against the 1980 Act requirements. This particular authority eventually acknowledged this and gave way to individual parents who wanted to apply in the second round to schools which were not on the list.

In the non-catchment-area authorities, the number of schools which a parent could choose from ranged from 2 to 35. Approximately one-third of these areas offered parents a choice from all the schools in the locality, whilst another third offered a choice from all the schools in the LEA. The remaining third indicated other factors which influenced the number of schools parents could choose from. These were: (a) links with contributory primary schools; (b) a pass or fail in the 11+ selection procedure; (c) the sex of the child; and (d) denominational or Welsh language requirements.

Having said that these areas offered parents several schools to choose from, Chapter 6 indicates that a number of parents living in a 'free choice' area did not feel at all advantaged because other factors limited the options open to them. This raises an important point, since by categorizing LEAs as 'catchment area' or 'non-catchment area', this suggests that the first group does little to acknowledge parental preference whilst the second group does. However, the following aspects of admissions procedures indicate how catchment-area policy is not by itself the most influential in the amount of choice parents have.

Timetable of Dates

The Education (School Information) Regulations 1981 state that LEAs have an obligation to publish general information and details of admission arrangements in advance of the year to which they relate and 'not later than six weeks before the date up to which parents may express a preference for a school'. Beyond this it is up to individual authorities to organize their own timetable of admissions arrangements. It seems that most areas do not publish the closing date for expressing a preference in their LEA brochure, but give this information in an accompanying letter or at some other time. The general pattern seems to suggest a fairly wide spread of closing dates among areas, which ranged from September through to May, although the majority of authorities with catchment areas were between December and April, whilst those without catchment areas tended to be slightly earlier – between November and March.

One authority asked for parental response in September – one year before transfer. It explained that this was necessary because it had a comprehensive and a selective system co-existing, and had therefore to ascertain which system parents preferred before organizing the 11+ selection procedure. At the other extreme, two authorities which left it as late as May to elicit parents' responses were both rural authorities which had never had to organize an appeal and thus felt little pressure to hurry the procedure along.

Quite a number of those officers interviewed said that they had found it necessary, since the implementation of the 1980 Act, to bring all their dates forward by a few weeks in order to fit in the large number of appeals before the summer holidays, and even then they did not always manage to achieve this. Conversely, two LEA officers explained that they tried to ensure that their appeals were not held too early, since this would result in school places becoming available after appeals decisions had been made. Another authority which had tried to bring forward its dates by two weeks and failed to do so, found that this had been beneficial in the end, since it had meant that they were able to settle more applications without going to appeal. A few neighbouring London boroughs have synchronized their timetable of admissions procedures so that parents can apply across boroughs more easily and do not get confused with a range of deadlines.

For some areas, one of the main problems in organizing a timetable of admissions procedures seemed to be the confusion as to whether or not it was acceptable legal practice to publish a closing date by which appeals must be filed. Those areas which decided that this was not permissible did not publish a date and some found in consequence that the scheduling of appeals was immensely difficult. The many areas which published such a date usually used it for administrative purposes only, i.e. to ensure that the majority of parents would respond by a certain time, and did not enforce it if one or two parents applied later than this date. However, in one LEA where the date was binding, the education officer dealing with appeals explained that the clerk to the appeals had interpreted the 1980 Act to mean that it would be illegal to hear an appeal after the main round of these was over. In actual fact, Schedule 2, Part II, to the Education Act 1980 states:

11. Subject to paragraphs 5 to 10 above, all matters relating to the procedure on appeals . . . including the time within which they are to be brought, shall be determined by the authority or governors by whom the arrangements are made. (See Appendix 2.4)

This is reinforced by the Council on Tribunals' 1985 Code of Practice which states:

An appeal should be lodged within the period specified by the authority or governors, as the case may be, but that period should not be less than 14 days from the notification of the decision; provision may be made for this period to be extended in exceptional circumstances.

ACC, 1985

Transport

Earlier in this chapter attention was drawn to the high proportion of urban areas which were using catchment areas. Perhaps more notable however are the six rural areas which initially invited parents to express a preference, i.e. were operating as free choice areas (see Table 3.1). However, despite the absence of defined catchment areas, 'natural' catchment areas had emerged, not only because of distances between rural schools, but also because authorities paid for travel to only one school – often to the nearest one or to the one which was appropriate in view of local transport arrangements. Approximately 30 per cent of the 125 LEA questionnaire respondents indicated that transport problems were among the major factors conflicting with the implementation of parental choice. Tables 3.2 and 3.3 give the range of travel arrangements made by local authorities as determined from their general information brochures. (N.b. The information in these tables was derived from the LEA booklets, not from the LEA questionnaire responses – hence numbers add up to 97, not 125.)

As one might expect, the most common practice in the sample of authorities with catchment areas was for the LEA to consider paying for transport only to the designated, catchment-area school, although four areas paid for transport to any school over three miles and one paid transport to any school over two miles. However, in authorities without catchment areas per se, it was also common practice to consider only paying for transport to the 'local' or designated school – thus implying a catchment-area school (Table 3.2). This was one of the main reasons why many parents living in non-catchment-area authorities still felt that they did not have a real option when choosing a school (see Chapter 6). Of course, parents who can afford to pay for, or provide, their own transport are not disadvantaged by this system, but for the majority of parents it is a major obstacle to choice.

Table 3.3 again shows that the majority of areas in our sample offered transport to the local or designated school only. Whilst Table 3.2 showed slight variations depending on whether or not the authority was organized into catchment areas, Table 3.3 demonstrates that 74 per cent of rural areas, compared with 54 per cent of urban areas, offered transport to the local school only. When looking at those authorities which pay for transport to *any*

in authorities with and without catchment areas

described in LEA booklets in urban, rural and urban/rural mixed authorities

	Authorities with catchment areas		Authorities without catchment areas		TOTAL	
	N	%	N	%	N	%
No transport provided	0	0	1	2	1	1
If over 3 miles to local or catchment area or designated school	39	71	17	40	56	58
If over 3 miles to nearest school with places available	4	7	8	19	12	12
If over 2 miles to local or catchment area or designated school	3	5	3	7	6	6
If over 3 miles to any school	4	7	9	21	13	13
If over 2½ miles to any school	0	0	2	5	2	2
If over 2 miles to any school	1	2	0	0	1	1
No transport provided, except where over 3 miles to a grammar or denominational school	1	2	0	0	1	1
Provision not indicated in booklet	3	5	2	5	5	5
TOTAL	55	99	42	99	97	99

	Urban		Rural		Mixed		TOTAL	
	N	%	N	%	N	%	N	%
No transport provided	1	2	0	0	0	0	1	1
If over 3 miles to local or catchment area or designated school	29	52	23	72	4	44	56	58
If over 3 miles to nearest school with places available	4	7	3	9	4	44	11	11
If over 2 miles to local or catchment area or designated school	3	5	3	9	1	11	7	7
If over 3 miles to any school	11	20	2	6	0	0	13	13
If over 2½ miles to any school	2	4	0	0	0	0	2	2
If over 2 miles to any school	1	2	0	0	0	0	1	1
No transport provided, except where over 3 miles to a grammar or denominational school	1	2	0	0	0	0	1	1
Provision not indicated in booklet	4	7	1	3	0	0	5	5
TOTAL	56	101	32	99	9	99	97	99

(percentages expressed within authority type)

school over a specified distance only 4 per cent (2) of rural areas do so compared with 19 per cent (13) of urban areas. Clearly, both local transport facilities, and the smaller distances involved in urban areas, make this a more viable procedure than in rural areas.

Intended Intakes

One of the requirements of the 1980 Act is that local authorities publish 'the number of pupils that it is intended to admit in each school year to each school to which the arrangements relate' (1980 Act, section 8(3): see Appendix 2.3). However this was not new to LEAs since the 1978 Education Bill had already proposed the idea of 'planned admissions limits' – a term which many local authorities still used when describing intended intake figures.

The intended intake figure indicates the maximum number of pupils the LEA intends to admit to each school, and is a figure which authorities must calculate for themselves, using whatever criteria they see fit, providing that the number of places does not fall by 20 per cent or more of the number of places that were available in 1979. Furthermore, LEAs are under no obligation to exceed their intended intake figures, even if the school has room to cater for more pupils, unless required to do so by the statutory appeal committee or the Secretary of State for Education under section 68 of the 1944 Act. Clearly this means that an LEA's policy towards calculating this arbitrary figure is crucial to the amount of choice parents have when expressing a preference for a certain school in their authority. For example, an LEA which operates a linked primary/secondary system and which sets each secondary school's intended intake figure to correspond exactly with the number of pupils in the final year of the contributory schools, leaves no scope for parents outside that linked system to opt in, unless parents of children already within that system opt out. Even in authorities without catchment areas or linked systems, intended intakes could be set sufficiently tightly and coupled with 'proximity' as an admissions criterion in order to have few places left after giving priority to those living near the school.

When asked what were the main factors conflicting with parental choice, 39 per cent (49) of 125 LEA area respondents indicated that the intended intake figures or the balancing of numbers between schools was a significant factor. One local education officer described section 6, which deals with parental preferences, and section 8, which deals with the setting of intended intakes, as the 'tension' in the 1980 Act.

The LEA questionnaire asked authorities on what basis they calculated their intended intakes. Although it has already been noted that there is no requirement that these necessarily correspond with the physical capacity of the school, 34 per cent (42) of areas replied that they actually used this criterion as the basis for their calculations. A further 29 per cent (36) of questionnaire respondents calculated their intended intakes on the total number of pupils about to transfer, divided in some way between schools. This it not to say that the total intended intake figure for all their schools was exactly that of the transfer cohort figure, because many authorities worked on the basis of rounding each school's numbers up to the nearest 30, i.e. the nominal size of a class, or up to the next staffing-allowance bracket. Some LEAs also deliberately added a few places specifically to leave scope for parental preferences. Indeed some authorities used previous years' intake patterns to calculate their intended intake figures, and in at least one instance the previous year's intake was taken as the new intended intake figure. Combined with falling rolls, this allowed for greater parental choice and provided a safeguard when managing staffing resources.

Many areas with falling rolls concentrated on protecting the viability of less popular schools by not allowing numbers in these schools to drop below a certain figure. In order to achieve this they often found it necessary to depress the intended intake figures in more popular schools so that places would have to be taken up in the less popular ones. When asked whether they considered this to be in line with meeting the demands of the 1980 Act and parental requests, one view which was frequently expressed was that the authority was protecting the rights of all parents by ensuring that pupils in less popular schools were not disadvantaged by being in a school which was gradually running down. Some officers also felt that local children should be assured of a neighbourhood school in future years. Clearly the only way this was possible was by ensuring that pupil numbers were sufficient to allow for adequate staffing, breadth of curriculum and facilities.

A large number of areas commented that the intended intake figures were not in themselves particularly detrimental to parental choice, but only became so when combined with falling rolls and the government requirement upon LEAs to reduce surplus places. (DES Circular 2/81 requires authorities to remove 20 per cent of the surplus places that arise between 1979 and 1986.) The important factor then becomes how an authority decides to reduce these spare places, if indeed it does anything about them at all. Some authorities elected to leave surplus places for the time being to allow parental choice trends to make their decisions for them; in other words to allow schools which were unpopular to reduce gradually until it became necessary to close them. One officer commented that this was not his wish, but that his education committee was determined to facilitate choice, even if this meant that a popular school was making another school virtually unviable. Often local councils were reluctant to make decisions on school closures because of political sensitivities; thus they preferred to go along with parents' wishes and close unpopular schools.

Another authority seemed to have solved its surplus places problem, and to have protected all of its schools, by giving each of the schools a turn at having their intake reduced by one form of entry, for one year only. In this way each school would not suffer such significant staffing or resource cuts because their numbers would only drop every third or fourth year (depending on the number of schools in town) and rose again the following year. Clearly the steps taken to deal with the problem of falling rolls depend very much on how rapidly numbers are decreasing, how low they are expected to drop, and whether they are expected to rise again in future years.

Many authorities had already taken out surplus places by merging or closing schools, so that the intended intake figure in their remaining schools once again related much more closely to the capacity of the buildings. Other LEAs said that they could not afford to close schools because when rolls started to increase again, they would have to reopen them. Thus, these authorities preferred to reduce places in several schools so that fluctuations in local population could be dealt with on an annual basis.

The margin between the total intended intake figures and the size of the transfer group was found to vary between 3 per cent and 30 per cent of the cohort, although one authority which was awaiting council decisions on reorganization and closures had a margin of 44 per cent in 1984! (These decisions have now been shelved until

1986, pending the outcome of local elections.) Needless to say, in this authority, all parents received their first choice, although the smallest school had an actual intake of only 95 which caused the authority some concern over its future. The surplus places were not actually staffed in this authority's schools – nor was there any evidence in other authorities to suggest that intended intake figures provided a basis for staffing allocation to schools.

Fairly large margins of around 20 per cent in other authorities were often found where an area had reduced its intended intake figures as far as possible (i.e. 19.9 per cent) without having to publish notices on the school and possibly then having to secure approval from the Secretary of State (1980 Act, section 15). Other areas were actually awaiting ministerial decisions on school closures or reductions of over 20 per cent, or had had these refused on various grounds. However, not all authorities had high margins because of such restrictions; a number chose to keep the margin between pupil numbers and intended intakes fairly wide in order to allow for parental preferences to be met. Indeed some officers expressed a view that to publish intended intake figures which were below the capacity of the school was immoral.

Areas with smaller margins between their cohort size and total intended intake figures claimed either to be deliberately restricting choice, or else had arrived at such a figure by rounding up catchment-area numbers to the nearest 30. One London borough said that their margin was in fact much greater than it appeared because many of its parents took up surplus places in 'more attractive' neighbouring authorities (the number of parents sending their children to schools outside this authority had risen from 10 per cent to 17 per cent in four years). Indeed, the officer said that the authority's plan to balance falling rolls between all its schools had back-fired for this very reason: parents who were refused a place in the school of their choice often did not accept a place in a less popular school, but transferred to a school outside the borough, which due to widespread falling rolls was becoming increasingly possible.

In discussions about intended intake figures, one final factor emerged which related to whether authorities ever refused a parent a place at a school which had not reached its published intake number. Whilst LEAs are not obliged to exceed the intended intake, to refuse to fill the school up to that number when the places are sought would seem to conflict directly with the spirit of the 1980 Act. Nevertheless a number of authorities said that there were circumstances in which they had not filled schools to their intended intake levels. Usually this had arisen when the admissions officers could not decide, on the basis of their published criteria, which of a number of pupils should be admitted where there were more pupils than places available (see next section). Thus, whilst some authorities would exceed their intended intake figures in these circumstances, others refused all applicants from outside the catchment area, and having provided details of the appeals procedure, decided to let the appeals panel decide about those parents who took their case that far. Another authority which had never had an appeal said that when a school was oversubscribed it was their policy either to admit all the applicants in a certain category (providing that this would not result in the need for extra staffing), or else to refuse all of them. For example, in 1984, a school in this authority had an intended intake of 182 and 153 catchment-area pupils had been accepted. Of the 59 out-of-area applicants, it took only 27, whereas to fill up to the intended admissions limit would have meant accepting 29 pupils. No parents appealed in this authority, but then it did not publish any criteria for admissions and so parents would not know whether they had been fairly refused or not.

Published Criteria

Besides requiring the publication of intended intake figures, the Education Act 1980 also requires local authorities to inform parents of 'the policy followed in deciding admissions' (section 8(3)(c): see Appendix 2.3), i.e. LEAs must list the criteria which they take into consideration when deciding on the merits of each parent's application for a school which is oversubscribed. These two aspects, intended intake figures and published criteria, provide the main framework in which LEAs can exercise their control over the amount of choice parents have. For example, in an LEA which has proximity to the school as its first criterion for admissions, a popular school will be likely to reach its intended intake on the basis of the first criterion alone, and parents living some distance from the school will be unable to secure a place. It should, of course, be noted that the criteria only come into operation when the number of applications for a school exceeds the intended intake figure. If the number of applicants is less than this figure and sections 6(3)(*b*) and (*c*) of the 1980 Act are not contravened then it follows that the parents' preferences must be met.

From an analysis of 97 brochures (see Table 3.4), it was found that the most common criterion was to do with siblings currently attending the secondary school (50), followed closely by catchment-area residence (43), medical factors (42) and proximity to the school (40). However while more authorities tended to take into account the criterion of siblings attending the school than any other factor, it was also apparent that this was more often given as the second criterion, preceded either by medical or catchment-area reasons.

Many LEAs gave overall priority to parents' first preferences, and in the first round of allocations would work through the published criteria, considering only these. Those parents who did not get their first preference by this route then had their second preference considered, again working through the published criteria, and so forth for third and subsequent preferences until all parents had been made an offer of a place. Some areas actually published 'Parents who name the school as first preference', as one of their admissions criteria. What was perhaps surprising was that single-sex or co-educational preferences featured so little in published criteria, and that 'educational reasons' were mentioned by only four areas. In two of these areas such reasons meant the desire for a particular course or subject. However, in the other two areas 'educational reasons' referred to the fact that a pupil attended a linked contributory school. Conversely, appeals panels, both formal and informal, were sometimes said to grant an appeal on the basis of a curriculum issue.

As Table 3.4 shows, many LEAs gave priority to children with older siblings already attending the school. It was notable that this was usually perceived by officers to be only fair, since they felt that most parents wanted all their children to attend the same school. However, when asked whether equal recognition would be given to parents who specifically requested a different school because of the sibling relationship, most authorities had either not considered this issue, or said that they would not give such a request the same priority. Whatever the situation here, the priority of siblings over children without older siblings at a school automatically reduces the

Table 3.4:   Ten most commonly cited criteria for deciding admissions in order of publication

Published criteria	1st criterion	2nd criterion	3rd criterion	4th criterion	5th criterion	6th criterion	TOTAL
	N	N	N	N	N	N	N
(a) Medical factors	25	10	5	1	1	–	42
(b) Catchment-area residents	23	10	9	1	–	–	43
(c) Siblings currently attending the school	15	30	2	3	–	–	50
(d) Sibling connection with the school (i.e. is or was attending it)	13	7	7	1	–	–	28
(e) Medical and/or social factors	3	2	5	1	–	–	11
(f) Distance to the school	3	8	17	8	3	1	40
(g) Attending feeder-primary school	1	4	4	3	3	–	15
(h) Denominational	–	–	6	5	2	–	13
(i) Out-borough children	–	–	1	5	2	3	11
(j) Single-sex or co-ed. preferences	–	1	2	2	4	–	9
TOTAL	83	72	58	30	15	4	262

N.b.   A further 37 criteria were found, although many were permutations of the above criteria and between them were only mentioned 70 times. (This information was obtained from the LEA booklets.)

rights or priority of access, and hence the choice, of parents of eldest or only children. In some authorities it was stated that the sibling priority would be disregarded subsequent to a parent requesting any school other than the one attended by older siblings – thus pressurizing parents to maintain the family link with a school. A similar effect can be observed with the criterion which gives priority to children attending 'linked' primary, junior or middle schools. In effect it enhances access to the local school whilst reducing the chances of getting into other schools. Whilst the educational arguments are strong (Stillman and Maychell, 1984), this criterion leads to a reduced choice for those parents whose children attend 'non-linked' primary schools. Two unfortunate by-products of the linking criterion have been described to the project. In the first, the linked contributory school can become popular solely for its secondary school admissions 'gate', a facet that upsets the balance of numbers between primary schools and the idea that the primary school is chosen on its own merit. The second problem relates to the difficulty of operating an education system when secondary school numbers are fixed by primary school intake figures six years earlier.

Perhaps the most crucial criterion with regard to choice is that of distance between home and school. It was often argued that this criterion was necessary if parents were to have protected or priority access to their local school, but this protection naturally results in reduced access to other schools. In a number of LEAs which did not have catchment areas, the distance criterion could be seen to bring about the same effect, but with more uncertainty than in catchment-area LEAs, since there is not a clearly defined boundary.

In some authorities distance was given a fairly low priority in the list of criteria. Another variation was to give priority to those parents whose next nearest school was further away than other parents' next nearest school. One LEA, when it cannot discriminate in any other way, literally pulls names out of a hat. Whilst this can be seen to offer equal choice to all, it does seem strange to base serious educational decisions on chance, although in this instance there are other criteria which come into play before the hat is used.

In general, authorities tended to list their criteria in order of priority, although some indicated that they gave equal priority to some or all of the criteria and a number omitted to mention whether the criteria were in order of importance or not. There was greater variation in the detail in which criteria were described: some brochures went to great lengths to give precise wording and listed up to ten criteria, whilst others failed to draw attention to the criteria by burying the information in prose form in the text, and by using broad generalizations. One authority said that it kept the criteria deliberately vague so that the parents could not engineer the system.

Eight authorities did not publish any criteria at all, which directly contravenes the requirements of the Education Act 1980. One such LEA said that they knew they were on difficult legal ground in not publishing their criteria, but they felt that this allowed them more flexibility, besides which they went to great lengths to meet parents' wishes – even to the point of putting in extra accommodation in one school and cutting it elsewhere. When, in another authority, the admissions officer was asked why his authority did not publish their criteria, he said that he felt it would be quite wrong to do so. He commented that the people sitting on the informal appeals panel used certain criteria, but that these did not need to be published beforehand. He added that the authority always granted the requests of parents who mentioned curriculum grounds as their reason for wanting a particular school. An officer in another area, when asked about published criteria said: 'We've not yet got to that stage, but we have talked about it'.

Uniformity/Diversity

So far, in considering catchment-area policies, intended admissions figures and published criteria, emphasis has been placed on the scope for choice depending on numbers of schools, places and pupils. However, choice not only relates to the quantity but also the quality of available options. Hence it is worth reflecting on the diversity of schools that parents are offered, and how far LEAs aim to maximize or minimize that diversity.

The project team asked each of the interviewed LEA officers (a) whether there were notable differences between schools in aspects such as the curriculum, teaching methods, etc., and (b) if the LEA had a policy of uniformity for its secondary schools, or if not, if this has ever been considered. When referring to the differences between schools, LEA officers tended to talk in terms of variations in popularity rather than of actual differences. By far the majority of comprehensive areas commented that the influence of ex-grammar schools was still important, often as much as 15 years after comprehensive reorganization, and that parents were attracted to what they perceived as 'the grammar school ethos'. One authority, which went comprehensive in 1974, had tried to remove 'labels' in parents' minds by renaming all the schools. However, the ex-grammar schools remained the most popular. For the same reason, another area closed both its grammar schools at the time of comprehensive reorganization: one went over to the private sector, whilst the other was made into a sixth-form college. This authority then put all its attention into converting its secondary modern schools into successful comprehensive schools without the problems of a lingering grammar school ethos in any of them. Conversely, a few authorities said that any trace of this phenomenon had disappeared quite naturally a long time ago, and that parents were more concerned these days about other issues such as a school's appearance, its curriculum and facilities.

A number of authorities perceived the headteacher as another influence on a school's popularity and in some areas LEAs had formulated policies on the appointment of their heads to deal with this. One LEA was not at all concerned that varying personalities and points of view among its headteachers would take the schools in different directions; indeed this was welcomed. Similarly in another, the officer commented 'we try to be non-interventionist; we encourage differences . . . and we rely on personality'. This seemed to be the most common viewpoint among authorities, although certainly not universal; one LEA officer said that due to a strict policy of uniformity among its secondary schools, headteachers' individualities had been 'stamped out' and noticeable similarities were to be found between heads who had been appointed since 1974. This same authority also concentrated upon establishing a common curriculum for its schools, and upon hearing at an appeal that a school was sought by a parent as the only one offering Latin to 11-year-old pupils, has since ensured that Latin is now available in several schools.

The main thrust of those LEAs which claimed to be seeking uniformity was the desire to ensure equality of educational provision. This involved additional money and advisory support for schools with poorer facilities and curriculum weaknesses. One authority said that this proved more economic than continually having to meet the excessive cost of overstaffing and subsidizing unpopular schools. Some areas, in an attempt to promote the uniformity that they believed in, had redrawn their catchment areas to ensure a comparable social mix in each school.

A small number of areas were found which aimed to promote diversity among their schools. These areas believed in encouraging each school's individual strengths, but for the most part appeared to be doing this through a policy of non-intervention rather than actively developing differences. One area officer described this as allowing diversity to evolve naturally, and another talked of encouraging schools to respond to local needs. For example, in this last authority one school had built up close links with local industries and was committed to a practical element in its fourth- and fifth-year syllabuses; another worked along the lines of a community school; and a third school concentrated particularly on those children with learning difficulties. Only one authority was found to have actively made decisions based on offering parents diversity, by ensuring variations in school size, single sex or mixed education, denominational and non-denominational schools, state and voluntary-aided education and so forth.

The question must also be raised about how the implementation of the 1980 Act has affected diversity between schools. If parents are expressing opinions, do these result in changes in the schools themselves? Obviously schools will be aware of popularity trends as reflected in their intakes, but many in the survey were uncertain about the reasons behind these figures. Whatever reasons parents offered, LEAs seldom conveyed these to the schools. They frequently commented that the reasons parents gave for wanting or not wanting a particular school were either irrelevant, unfounded or based upon the published criteria. Yet surely even parents' misconceptions about a school would be of interest to that school and might help it to adjust its public image? Without this feedback to schools, they will continue to have difficulty in responding directly to public opinion. One head said that he wrote to his LEA officers each year to ask why approximately 20 per cent of his catchment area annually opted away from the school, and had so far received no reply. He expressed frustration that where market forces were being allowed to operate, he was not allowed to know why parents were choosing not to buy from his stall. In some LEAs, however, all the school applications were dealt with at school level by the governors of each school. Whatever comments and reasons that were offered by the parents were seen by the governors. Currently this seems to be the only route by which schools can become aware of and, if necessary respond to, the more subtle aspects of parental choice.

Summary

The range of LEA practice described in this chapter indicates the extent to which local authorities, through their admissions policies and procedures, structure the amount of choice available to parents. Whilst the use of a 'free choice' system implies a certain attitude towards parents choosing their children's schools (an attitude which is sometimes borne out in practice), the absence of catchment areas does not, in itself, mean unrestricted choice. It would appear that other aspects, such as the provision of transport or the size of the intended intake figure exert a greater influence on how much choice parents have. Indeed, the range of choice between the various LEA situations could be viewed as a continuum with unhindered free choice at one end and tightly controlled catchment areas at the other, rather than as polarized 'types'.

Various features of LEA policy indicate at what point along this continuum an authority would be placed. For example, within those authorities operating catchment areas, factors such as the requirement of a reply from all parents or just from those who wish to state a preference for another school, the sending of a proforma for stating that preference or the requirement of a letter of application, the assurance to parents of a 'reserved' place or the withdrawal of that privilege if a preference is stated, all affect the type of choice offered. Similarly, in authorities without catchment areas, choice is limited not only by the number of schools a parent can choose from, but also by whether transport is paid to all, some, or just one of those schools.

Other features, such as intended intake figures transcend the catchment area or 'free choice' organization. When, in the latter, intended intake figures are closely related to the overall numbers of pupils transferring, choice will naturally be restricted and popular schools will become oversubscribed. When the authority then has to refer to its published criteria it is easy to see why the most common first criterion – 'proximity to the school' – will effectively divide 'free choice' LEAs into catchment areas. This will also apply where transport is only paid to one school.

Conversely, where the margin between intended intake limits and actual pupil numbers is wide, either because an LEA strongly supports parental choice or because it has not been able to reduce its surplus places sufficiently, then scope for parental choice will be far greater. As such, published criteria will be less influential in these areas since more parents will be offered the school of their choice without the LEA having to take the published criteria into consideration. However, transport arrangements are still crucial in these areas, since for the majority of parents choice is likely to remain theoretical if, by exercising that choice and being offered the school, they then have to pay for transport themselves.

Finally, the question of encouraging diversity or uniformity in schools is an interesting point, since advocates of each seem to believe that they are acting in support of the principle of parental choice. Those who support diversity clearly interpret choice to mean the provision of schools with different characteristics and strengths. Thus parents can choose on the basis of curriculum, attitudes to discipline and uniform, remedial work and so forth. Alternatively, those LEAs which encourage uniformity between schools seem mainly concerned with equality of provision. Thus they believe that only by ensuring that all schools are equally as good can all parents be offered a fair choice.

Although diversity in the form of schools developing their own curriculum strengths does not preclude developing uniformity of provision within schools, in practice it is interesting that the perceived means of achieving each of these aims varies from strong intervention, sometimes including policies on the appointment of headteachers, to laissez-faire policies on the basis that there is strength in individuality and that heads should develop their own school's strengths. The problem must remain, in either case, that the authority is responsible for the provision of education and that the desirability of various school features or qualities will continue to be debatable.

CHAPTER 4

The Provision of Information for Choice

> Without information it is not a choice but a lottery.
> William Shelton, House of Commons, 25th April 1975

The effective operation of choice and the need for information go hand in hand. Without the necessary information, choice of school is, as quoted above, no more than a lottery. For this reason section 8 of the 1980 Act and the Education (School Information) Regulations 1981 require certain minimum information about schools and about LEAs' admissions procedures to be published annually. In 1984, the project collected parents' booklets from 100 of the 104 LEAs in England and Wales and all of these published sufficient information to meet most if not all of the statutory requirements. Beyond this minimum level is where the enormous differences between LEAs became apparent.

Of course, information can be provided in many forms and parents will draw upon their own sources where they wish. For some, the school and LEA-produced materials will be unnecessary or even unwanted, but for others they could well represent the only sources of information available. This chapter deals specifically with the five main types of information provided by schools and LEAs: (1) the LEA booklet which provides the general information for parents; (2) the school brochures which include the published examination results; (3) the pre-choice visit to the secondary school; (4) talks about secondary schools held in the primary school; and (5) the primary school itself. It is recognized that few parents will have encountered all five of these sources and that in practice there is likely to be a degree of overlap amongst them, which may not always be constructive.

In seeking to assess the value of the information in the parents' decision making process, the project has neither set out to provide a linguistic analysis of printed materials nor to check up on their accuracy with respect to individual schools. Instead, the research was more concerned with the 'tone' of publications, how they facilitated choice, the intended scale of distribution and whether the information deliberately masked or highlighted school diversity. In the conclusion to this chapter two general questions will be addressed: are parents well served by the current levels of provision of information, and do the schools use the provision constructively to gain any other benefits that might accrue; for example, do the schools seek to involve the parents in the process of education? But these questions assume the provision of information to be politically neutral and perhaps a third question needs to be raised: is the nature of the information and the scale of its provision being used to influence the degree of parental involvement in the choice of school?

The LEA Booklet

The project invited every LEA in England and Wales to send a copy or copies of their general information booklets and 100 LEAs responded positively. This request was aimed at the publications LEAs are required to produce under section 8 (1), (2), (3) and (4) of the 1980 Act and Schedule 1 to the Education (School Information) Regulations 1981.

Of the 100 LEAs which responded, 68 used single publications to cater for all of the information needed for admission to secondary schools in their area. A further 16 authorities produced separate, parallel publications to cover LEA-wide and area information, and their 'parents' would thus receive the LEA-wide booklet and the appropriate local details. A final group of 16 LEAs published local booklets only. In all, 32 LEAs published local booklets of which 27 were large, rural or semi-rural LEAs where individual towns or cities were discrete from each other and likely to have separate systems dating back to before the 1974 reorganization. The other five were metropolitan authorities. In one of these, size may be seen as the reason for this localized provision, whilst in the other four local booklets reflected localized catchment areas. In all, the project collected 84 LEA-wide booklets and 240 local, or area booklets: a total of 324 publications in all.

Problems of Mis-Information

Unfortunately, the general information booklets did not always contain all the legally-required information. Many authorities enclosed a letter to the parents when their booklet was sent out just prior to the date for most parents to express their preference, and often, quite correctly, this letter contained some of the necessary information. However, when the booklet was requested at other times, for example, when parents had just moved into the area, the 'accompanying' letter was not always included. Whenever the project found omissions the LEAs concerned were contacted again, but the situation was not always remedied. In a number of instances legally-specified information was simply not published.

The absence of certain information represents an obvious problem for parents as their ability to participate in the process could be impaired. In some cases no one had thought to publish certain bits of information at all, and at least in one instance a conscious decision had been made to not publish them. The main omissions related to intended intake figures, which were omitted from 14 booklets, and admissions criteria, which were left out of six. Inaccuracies and ambiguities also occurred but somewhat less frequently. In several booklets the intended intake figure was called a 'Planned Admissions Limit', and in one instance a booklet also referred specifically to the 'Planned Operating Capacity' as the maximum number of pupils the LEA proposed to admit in that year of entry to each school. The difference is subtle, but certainly conveys an erroneous emphasis: both these terms derive from Labour's 1978 Education Bill which would have made exceeding these figures reason to refuse further admission. The Bill never became law and the current 'intended intake' figure has no 'power' of its own: it is just a guideline (see Chapter 2).

Parents living in London boroughs were often informed quite categorically in the general information booklets that admission to schools in neighbouring boroughs would only be possible after places had been found for all the pupils resident within those boroughs. This would appear to contradict the spirit of section 6(5) of the 1980 Act, which includes children from outside the LEA in the duty to comply with any preference and it certainly would appear to contravene section 31(8) of the London Government Act 1963 which states that:

. . . it shall not be a ground for refusing a pupil admission to, or excluding a pupil from, any such school or institution maintained or assisted by a local education authority in Greater London that the pupil resides in the area of some other local education authority if that area is within, or is contiguous with any part of, Greater London . . .

Whilst neither piece of legislation suggests that a London borough's own resident pupils should not be placed first, the refusal to place an out-borough pupil into the preferred school *solely* on the grounds that the child came from a different borough would seem to contravene the 1963 Act.

A similar preferential effect was achieved by at least two London boroughs which make residence in the borough either the first of the admissions criteria or part of each criterion. However, there was one London borough which afforded out-borough pupils the same rights as its own residents, but for its residents, reciprocal arrangements allowing ease of access into neighbouring boroughs did not seem apparent.

This sort of practice was also common outside London and indeed in some cases, preference even operated between areas within the LEA. In many ways it is surprising that the legislation does not require all LEAs to explain the 'new' (post-1980) position for cross-boundary applications. This issue is further confused because of the distinction that is made between 'special agreements' (which might exist for instance where two LEAs agree to a school drawing pupils from both sides of a county boundary) and individual choice. The regulations only require LEAs to give details of these special agreements and the impression can be given that where no agreements exist, parents have no rights to apply to schools in neighbouring LEAs. Typically, we see in one booklet that the only reference to cross-boundary applications, apart from saying that the parent would have to pay for the transport, was as follows:

The Local Education Authority has no standing arrangements to take up places at schools maintained by other Local Education Authorities or at non-maintained (independent) schools.

Whilst being technically correct, this can hardly be construed as fully informing parents of their rights. Similarly, if the 'assisted places scheme' is to operate fairly one might have thought that all parents should have been made aware of its existence. Reference to the scheme in LEA booklets was rather scant.

There were two other issues which could be misleading. The Act requires LEAs to publish 'the policy followed in deciding admission', and this is normally taken to include the admissions 'criteria'. For the most part the LEAs published these criteria as short lists and clearly stated whether any priority existed within the list (see Chapter 3). However, a few LEAs embedded their criteria in descriptive passages. As the whole concept of admissions criteria and how they are used is complicated, the potential for misunderstanding is high and it would thus seem sensible to present them as clearly and unambiguously as possible. The parent interviews also revealed that a number of parents believed that LEAs were using criteria other than those published in the booklets. Some of these 'other criteria' were simply outdated ones which were no longer in use whilst others had a kind of Machiavellian air. The published lists of criteria were presumably intended to be exclusive and no other criteria should have been in use. It would be helpful if this were made explicit.

In most booklets the details about LEAs' (statutory) appeals systems were reasonably presented albeit they were somewhat legalistic in their phrasing which might militate against parents understanding them. Some LEAs included full details in these general booklets whilst others provided separate publications which were referred to in the general booklet. However, in a number of instances the details of an authority's admissions procedure and its non-statutory, internal appeals or 'reviews' merged with the descriptions of their statutory appeals system. There were booklets which implied that the statutory appeals would not consider medical evidence submitted after the closing date for preferences, and in one case a booklet read as if the parents' right to appeal was to be met by the chief education officer reviewing their case. The two types of appeal had unfortunately merged and the information had become confused.

The Style and Presentation

Overall the LEA booklets tended to be dull and unappealing, with only a few authorities using imaginative layouts and attractive, welcoming language. A number were notable for their economy. Typewritten formats were common and the advent of the 'shrinking' photocopier has permitted some drastic miniaturization. For all this it surely must be the tone of the booklet that counts the most. The least encouraging publications tended to emphasize the LEA and governors' role in deciding school admissions, and parental preference was only mentioned as a kind of unfortunate legal necessity. In other instances a well-written and balanced introduction seemed to give a fair and attractive appraisal of the position. The introduction for one authority read as follows:

Parents have the right to express a preference for one or more schools. Most will probably want to send their child to a school close to home, but some may prefer a different school. Whatever your preference, we will try to meet it, but there will be cases where this proves impossible because there is a limit to the number of new pupils a school can take in each year. If we cannot meet your preference for a school, you will have an opportunity to discuss other possibilities with us and if you are still unhappy, you can appeal against our decision.

In another example we can see not only the positive attitude and the use of clear, easy language but also an encouragement to visit the schools.

We shall do all we can to enable your child to go to the secondary school you prefer and this is what happens for most children. But some schools have more children wanting to go there than there is room for and so we have to ask some parents to make a second preference. I hope your child will be one of the majority who gain a place first time, but if not, and you are asked to choose another school from those in which vacancies still exist, please go and see these schools and talk to the heads. Don't dismiss them out of hand. Go and judge them for yourself.

On the other hand there are authorities which present a negative attitude. One authority, after quoting section 6 of the 1980 Act went on to give the education committee's view . . .

> The Education Committee's view is that there are many educational and social advantages in children attending their local schools and, therefore, places are normally provided for children of all ages in the local schools serving the areas in which they live.
>
> At the same time, however, it is the Committee's policy to meet the wishes of parents about schools their children attend whenever it is both possible and reasonable to do so. In order that such requests may be considered, the Committee have laid down the following conditions which must be satisfied:
>
> a) the proposed school must be, in academic terms, appropriate and suitable for the child concerned;
> b) the Planned Admission Limit for the school must not be exceeded by the admission of the child;
> c) parents must accept responsibility for the daily travelling arrangements, including costs; and
> d) the wishes of the parents must not run counter to the Authority's clear objectives of providing an efficient education service and using its limited resources efficiently.
>
> Parents should note that the relevant sections of the Education Act 1980 (principally Sections 6–8) provide for parents to have a statutory right to *express a preference* for the school they wish their child to attend: the sections do not provide for a 'freedom of choice' for parents.

The 'legalistic', anti-choice writings continued for a few more lines but the message was clear. What is more the message would appear to contain passages that would be difficult to defend in court. The four conditions that the committee in the above example has decided need to be met before it will *consider* an application have no legal standing. Parents can apply for schools whatever the position of the four clauses above. Assuming the request is submitted at the right time the authority must not only consider it, but also decide upon it, and parents can then appeal if they wish.

These three examples serve to illustrate the range of approaches used by authorities to inform parents of their potential role in school allocations. We can see how the booklet's attitude might influence parents' subsequent actions. Since for many parents the LEA's general information booklet serves as their only 'official' source of information and guidance, its potential influence should not be underestimated.

Patterns of Distribution

The general information booklets are sent out to all parents whose children are due to be admitted to secondary school in the following year and as far as we could determine this distribution occurred in all cases by the booklets being sent home from the primary school via the child. The reason for this complete distribution arises out of section 5(4)(*b*) of the Education (School Information) Regulations 1981. Where parents wanted booklets for other areas they were made available at no charge from the appropriate education offices; there was however some indecision amongst education officers about whether the parent might have to pay for the postage. For people other than parents the Regulations only require copies to be available for reference, although many authorities still send them out upon request.

Translations into Other Languages

A number of the booklets contained translations or were available separately in different languages. The most noticeable, numerically, were the Welsh versions, but translations were also seen in Punjabi, Bengali, Hindi, Gujerati and Urdu, though perhaps less commonly than one might have expected. The majority of these translations were provided for parts of the booklet only, and this seemed discriminatory as they contained less than the complete English description. However, in other cases the partial translation was potentially supplemented by the provision of the telephone number of an interpreter at the authority's offices, or the name and address of someone to contact.

An alternative approach to informing non-English speaking parents was to bring direct assistance to the parents in the primary school, and in one authority the personnel from a language unit made themselves available at special meetings. However, a large number of the authorities we spoke to did nothing to assist non-English speaking parents. Often it was said that there was no need since there were no non-English speaking families in their schools, and this would be allied to there being no special language provision being made available in the primary schools or the fact that nobody had actually asked the authority for a translation. Alternatively authorities commented that if there were any problems they would be handled by the primary school teachers who already knew the parents, or by the children who would, by now, be able to read English. In neither case were we told of any moves by these LEAs to check whether their approach was appropriate, nor whether they had fully appreciated the inherent difficulties and loss of accuracy that occurs when children translate for their parents.

One authority took a radically different view. They refused to publish translations on the grounds that they would have to print so many that it would be too expensive. They relied upon the local ethnic communities to provide their own translations.

The Regulations are very open on this point. It is up to the LEA to decide if a translation is required: no criteria are offered (section 8(4), Education (School Information) Regulations 1981). Obviously there is a problem of additional cost for the authorities if extra printing is involved. However, the insertion of brief passages in the more popular of the non-English languages, giving minimum information and appropriate phone numbers, would not seem to be excessive. One example of this can be seen in this translation of a passage in Urdu given in one LEA's booklet (the passage was given in both Urdu and English):

Some parents of Pakistani origin who do not employ English as their only or main language may wish to discuss the contents of this booklet with someone who is fully aware of the Authority's policies on admissions to schools and who is fluent in Urdu. Mr —, Community Relations Officer and Co-opted member of the Education Committee has agreed to be available to discuss the contents of this booklet with you. He can be contacted at . . .

Additional School Information

Approximately one-fifth of all the booklets contained considerable information about the secondary schools in their area: information normally written by the schools and subsequently compiled and published by the LEA. These school descriptions presented considerably more information than just the schools' names and addresses, as required by the Regulations, but the requirements of brevity and common formats tended to make the similarities outweigh the differences. As a result, although these descriptions were informative, they still seemed more likely to reassure parents that all the schools were suitable than to encourage discrimination. For some education officers, though, these booklets were only intended as 'tasters': the real information being available only from visiting the school.

Publishing booklets like this had one distinct advantage over conventional school brochures in that they were sent to all the parents in the LEA or area. In this sense a 'message' from each school was almost guaranteed to reach each parent and thus widen the information horizon beyond the decreed or practised catchment area (see Chapter 3 for a discussion on catchment areas). As far as we could ascertain, the inclusion of school information in the LEA booklet did not occur at the expense of the individual school brochures, which is perhaps appropriate, since the two publications serve very different purposes.

The School Brochure

The project made no systematic attempt to collect school brochures but over time amassed some 164 booklets, leaflets and information sheets. From this small and unrepresentative collection of brochures, and from the discussions with schools and LEAs, several patterns relating to the contents and distribution of school brochures have emerged.

As with the LEA general information booklets, the school brochures are a legal requirement. Schedule 2 to the Education (School Information) Regulations 1981 lays down the minimum information content which for English secondary schools should include, amongst other things, details or descriptions of the type of school; religious affiliations; the curriculum; subject choices and the levels to which they are taught; sex, careers and special education; the school's organization including pastoral care, discipline and societies; the public examinations' policy and the latest results; and the uniform policy and the cost of each item. A moment's scrutiny of this list, though, will show how difficult it is, even with a comprehensive list of features, to provide appropriate and efficient school descriptors to help parents select the school that most suits them.

Beyond this, school brochures suffer two further problems. First there is almost bound to be an element of 'public relations' in some brochures, and probably very rightly. But some parents are sceptical of 'PR' and faced with any brochure will believe that the schools are putting a 'gloss' on everything. The second problem is more fundamental. Whether it be through official LEA directives, LEA approval of cartel arrangements, or simply tacit acceptance of 'gentlemen's agreements' between heads, many schools seem to be neither trying to sell themselves nor emphasizing particular policies or characteristics. Within any one area the brochures often tended to be more similar than one might expect and in some sets of brochures, individual school initiative had disappeared. In its place the sets tended to favour the most economic format and seemingly, for comparative use, i.e. for choosing between schools, the least informative approach. This was particularly apparent when LEAs printed the brochures for the schools and produced series of 'clones'. With some sets of brochures, if the actual names and addresses were deleted it would be difficult, if not impossible, to identify the schools by their educational descriptions alone. However this was not always the case and in one authority in 1984, £25,000 was spent producing professionally printed, interesting and varied school brochures.

There are, unfortunately, many difficulties here, not the least being that schools are not always easily and usefully distinguishable, i.e. what can be distinguished is not always useful for the purposes of choosing. Furthermore, to emphasize differences may be to contradict the LEA policy of providing schools which are equally capable of catering for all the potential educational needs in the community. There is however at least one LEA which claims to positively encourage individual initiatives so that the school's philosophy can 'shine through'.

School Examination Results

As is mentioned above, all secondary schools' examination results are required to be published. When this issue first arose it attracted considerable attention and debate and many argued that a measure of the output alone told the reader little about the quality of the process. Similarly it was felt that exams were only one part of a school's work and hence the publication of the results focused attention away from the other aspects. Furthermore, as teachers and children change from year to year, the presentation of just one year's results was going to be too varied and unstable to be of use (see Plewis *et al.*, 1981). In practice the actual publication of the results is sporadic and, among parents, interest in them is seemingly low. Many parents we talked to did not even know that they were meant to be published (see Chapters 5 and 6). Where we saw copies, often as separate insertions in the brochures, they tended to follow the Regulations closely, but that does not reduce the difficulties described above.

Publishing Information in the Press

Many parents reported seeing the examination results in the local papers, and in some instances more parents saw the results in the press than in brochures (see Chapters 5 and 6). Some authorities and groups of schools recognize this and make a point of providing the press with the results in a 'useful' and fair form. However, in many instances the press can only publish odd bits and pieces and in some areas the heads will not provide any details at all. If the local press is seen as a useful medium for reaching parents, and a number of LEAs publish allocation procedures and open evening dates in it, and many schools 'sell' themselves through its weekly columns, then it would seem useful to use the medium constructively.

Non-Educational Differences

The question of non-educational differences between schools provides similar difficulties. Is it sensible that the bright, new school on an owner-occupier estate should advertize its situation at the expense of its urban-decayed neighbour, and for how long should the ex-grammar be allowed to feature this aspect at the expense of the ex-secondary modern? Having criticized the 'cloned' nature of some LEAs' schools brochures they may now be seen as protecting schools, and consequently upholding a choice for those parents who want their children to go to the local school.

Other Benefits from the Brochures

School brochures can also be used to enhance parental involvement in their child's education and to encourage greater school accountability. A well-written, thorough and attractively laid-out school brochure might well persuade the parents to enter into the process of their child's education and there are brochures which face up to this challenge well, which put the school in a good light and which are inviting to the parents.

There is a necessary distinction to be drawn here between that information published solely to satisfy the 1980 Act and that which schools publish to their enrolled but still prospective parents, and there are those who would argue that it is too costly to produce separate documents to satisfy both demands. One of the solutions the project encountered was to spend very little time or money on the 1980 Act brochure and then to provide an attractive school magazine in June or July – a magazine which would be circulated only to the parents of enrolled children. But any analysis of the information required to meet the two different demands should reveal that there is little in the 1980 Act brochure that is not normally provided in the school magazine, and some of the better (1980 Act) brochures have more than adequately catered for both purposes and thus removed the need for the second publication. There seem to be two reasons why catering for both demands is not more universal: first, the cost of 'pre-choice' distribution can exceed the cost of distributing only to 'enrolled' parents, and secondly, this wider distribution might be seen as 'poaching', something which goes against the gentleman's agreements mentioned before.

Patterns of Distribution

With school brochures, the patterns of distribution are as important as the quality and depth of the information provided. Unlike the LEA's general information booklet, there is no legal requirement for school information to be sent out unless requested, though in practice many, but not all, LEAs tend to encourage some form of automatic distribution. The project encountered three typical patterns of school brochure distribution.

In the first instance, the distribution was virtually non-existent. A minimal 'brochure' was typed and kept in the head's desk. If any parent asked for a copy (and in fairness, apparently, this was a very rare event for some schools) the one top copy was photocopied. Occasional handwritten amendments were made from year to year to cope with small changes and, if provided, the examination summary was annually updated. Technically this probably met the legal requirements, but little more.

The second pattern occurred where school brochures were produced in time for 'choice' but were only distributed to catchment-area pupils. Any suggestion of a brochure going beyond its catchment area was described as 'poaching' and it is apparent that this was a contentious issue in many areas. Copies were, however, available to parents from outside the school's catchment area.

The third distribution pattern commonly occurred where all the schools in an area held open evenings. The brochures were not distributed in advance, but they were made available on these evenings. They were also available by post or for collection to any parent who specifically asked at a later date. In many of these cases the LEA also published a brief description of each school in its general information booklet and hence all parents received some information: those who attended the open evenings received much more.

When the project met with schools and LEAs to discuss the distribution and style of school brochures, teachers and officers often argued that the publications should not give parents false hopes about choice and that this publicity costs money which could be better spent on actually educating the pupils. As has already been suggested, the first of these arguments assumes choice to be the only reason for producing school brochures, which is really not the case, although it may well be that a number of schools have little interest in achieving either greater parental involvement or accountability and so may perceive the brochures as fulfilling only the one function.

The issue of restricted distribution on the grounds of avoiding poaching or of giving false hope is difficult. If there is only one school for 50 miles then the false hope argument is most reasonable and poaching would not arise. If, however, the false hope arises because the LEA policy is towards containment through the operation of catchment areas or the use of distance as an admissions criterion, then distribution is being restricted in order to disguise, or to support, an LEA policy. Similarly the poaching argument has difficulties in that it presupposes that a school has rights to its catchment residents and therefore other schools should not trespass. The parents' own rights are given little consideration in this approach, and this poaching argument would seem directly to counter the spirit of the 1980 Act.

The problem of cost to schools is very real and inescapable: printed brochures are expensive and many schools are given no extra assistance. However, many authorities seemed keen to help schools with this problem. Approximately one-quarter of the authorities we talked to printed the brochures for the schools in the council's own printroom, though the reasons for this were often more to do with a combination of achieving both uniformity and economy, than with generosity towards the schools. Alternatively other types of support could be given. One LEA simply paid for all the brochures to be professionally printed, whilst others gave money either in lump sums or as amounts per brochure. For example, one LEA offered schools up to 25p per brochure up to a limited number of copies. Other kinds of material assistance were also made available, with one LEA offering up to 30 hours' secretarial time and several others offering paper.

Many examples of both good and bad features of school brochures have been compiled by the Scottish Consumer Council in an attempt to help schools produce the better kind of brochure described above (Atherton, 1982). The National Consumer Council is due to produce a similar publication for England and Wales. (See also *School Prospectus Planning Kit* by Felicity Taylor (ACE, 1980) and *Written Communication Between Home and School* edited by John Bastiani (1978).)

Pre-Choice Visits to Secondary School

Many parents have told us that the only way to find out about a school is to go and visit it. The small number of parents we have met who had had guided tours during working hours have tended to be most enthusiastic about this way of seeing the school and praised the opportunity it presented to talk about the school with the head or teachers in small groups. In practical terms though the daytime visit of perhaps only three or four parents at a time is unrealistic if many parents request it: few schools can afford the amount of time and not all parents can take time off work. One compromise is to open the school for an evening sometime prior to the parents actually having to state their preference; a practice that has become fairly widespread (see Table 4.1).

A total of 58 per cent of the LEA questionnaire respondents reported that 'all' or 'most' of their secondary schools held open days or evenings prior to the parents having to register their preference. (For simplicity both open days and evenings will be referred to as open evenings from now on.) But school open

Table 4.1:   **The LEA-reported incidence of school open days or evenings prior to the initial allocation of places (Q5 on LEA questionnaire)**

Number of schools in area holding open evenings	Response for catchment area		Response for 'free choice' area		Response for all areas	
	N	%	N	%	N	%
All	21	28	22	45	43	34
Most	17	22	13	26	30	24
Some	17	22	8	16	25	20
None	8	11	3	6	11	9
Unknown	7	9	2	4	9	7
No response	6	8	1	2	7	6
TOTAL	76	100%[1]	49	100%[2]	125[3]	100%

Notes
[1] 100% represents approximately 1440 schools
[2] 100% represents approximately 88 schools
[3] The project received completed questionnaires from 125 areas. See Chapter 3 for further details of this survey and Appendix 3:1 for how to obtain details about the 'areas' reported upon.

evenings are not required by any statute and it is apparent that their occurrence reflected the LEA's school admissions' policy. Thus, whilst they occurred in 'all' or 'most' schools in 35 out of 49 free choice areas, this proportion drops to 38 out of 76 in catchment areas. At the other extreme, in eight out of 76 catchment areas no schools held open evenings and, perhaps surprisingly, the same is true of three out of the 49 free choice areas.

Although many respondents (44 per cent) reported that 'some' or 'most' of their schools held open evenings, the project's experience in a limited number of instances suggests that the distribution of schools holding open evenings was not random amongst those that did not. The frequent references we heard to 'touting', 'poaching' and 'gentlemen's agreements' were sufficient to indicate that neighbouring schools considerably influence each other's behaviour. Accordingly it would seem unlikely that there would be schools holding open evenings near to others which did not: the latter schools would want to change the situation although the change might take a number of years to effect. If, however, there were several discrete groups of schools within an area, perhaps centred in several different towns, then it is perfectly reasonable to suppose that all the schools in some groups would hold open evenings whereas in other groups none of them would.

Typically the open evenings held before the closing date for stating a preference had three elements: the tour, the questioning and the talk. The easiest system for the tour seemed to be for the teachers and pupils to stay in certain places around the school and for the parents to wander freely. Maps and signposts are necessary but the parents can pace their own tour. With classrooms and laboratories open, and pupils' work displayed, many parents passed through without talking to teachers en route, thus leaving easy access for those who wanted to ask specific questions of the appropriate teachers. Much of the information sought was such that the one-to-one situation was better than had the parent been in a large group, and equally, the direct access to specialists allowed better and more confident answers than might have been the case if answered by the head or deputy.

In some of the evenings we saw parents taken around the school by either teachers or pupils. The problems of guided tours – grouping the parents, of keeping them together, and giving multiple talks in the hall, seemed to outweigh the advantages. From the parents' point of view this system has little to offer, especially since it virtually precludes the opportunity to talk to more than one teacher.

In both systems starting and finishing the talks seemed problematic, since latecomers were often still arriving long after the first of the early leavers had left. The solution is not straight-forward. To hold the talk at the beginning of the evening is to increase the number who arrive late, whilst if it is held at the end of the evening, greater disruption will occur from those who leave early. A further problem arose from poor sound amplification and in a number of cases the person giving the talk was inaudible.

In spite of these problems, the talks and subsequent question sessions were interesting and seemingly appreciated by the parents, and, furthermore, they allowed the heads to emphasize the participation between the school and parents more strongly than they might have done in the brochure. In most cases this and other strongly held philosophies were very well put over. In some talks the heads also introduced a number of their staff and asked them to talk briefly about one or more issues. Whilst this might demonstrate the head's confidence in his or her teachers and provide a different voice for the parents to listen to, it also encouraged the talks to go on too long and to become repetitious.

Where the schools were keen to present themselves, the parents were also enthusiastic about asking difficult questions. As one might expect there were questions about examination results, banding, intake numbers, amounts of homework, out-county applications and so forth. Heads were also challenged about whether their mixed schools would be as good for girls as single-sex schools were argued to be, and furthermore, a number were asked to describe and effectively defend their policy on streaming or mixed ability. The overall impression was that many parents take an active interest in the technical aspects of their children's education. A number of schools reinforced this view by suggesting that one outcome of the 1980 Act has been the enhanced level of questioning by parents that has taken place since the Act was implemented in 1982.

At the open evenings we attended there were many primary school age children present and the evenings were, to a large extent, their evenings as well as the parents'. For many parents the child's feelings are an important consideration in the choice of school (see

Chapter 6), and therefore it makes sense for the child as well as the parents to see the schools. The involvement of the child in the choice of school was plainly evident from the many snippets of parent/child conversation, and the explanations and questions were flowing both ways. In one of the schools the children's presence was keenly felt at the end of the formal talk (about 9.45 p.m.) when the head asked for questions. In between the parents' questions and in front of several hundred people, ten-year-old children were able to ask about homework and sport, and they received straightforward and mostly non-patronizing answers.

The question of whether children should be allowed or encouraged to attend is clear-cut in the ideal situation. If their involvement in the choice of school is sought, then it seems sensible to allow them to see the schools before the choice is made. The choice still belongs to the parents, but the child can usefully and meaningfully participate in its making and so also partake in any subsequent involvement and commitment. At a more mundane level, it was also apparent that some parents had had to bring their children with them as they could not be left at home alone. If children had not been allowed then these parents could not have attended. However, the presence of children can add to a space problem: some of the open evenings were seriously cramped and for this reason one LEA actually refused to admit children to its schools' open evenings.

Secondary Talks in Primary School

In some instances secondary school staff visited their main contributory primary schools to speak to parents there rather than inviting them to the secondary school. In many respects these occasions were very similar to the formal talk-and-question sessions of the secondary open evening except that they tended to be much smaller, with perhaps only 10 to 20 parents present.

Whilst the talk and questioning could be lively and informative, these evenings lacked the tour round the secondary school and in this respect they were not as good as the full open evening. They seemed to be held, though, in areas where the open evening might have been regarded as poaching whilst the restricted-audience talk was taken as acceptable. For the staff involved it inevitably became a bit of a travelling show, with perhaps five or six talks spread over two weeks. For the parents, knowledge of the secondary school was gained at second hand.

It is sometimes argued by heads that holding these evenings at the primary school brings in more parents than would be the case at the secondary school simply because the parents know where to go and the primary school is probably nearer to home. However, in urban areas at least, there is ample evidence of parents turning out in large numbers to secondary school open evenings when invited (see Chapters 5 and 6).

The Primary School Influence

The publication of information six weeks prior to the expression of choice and the emphasis on open evenings and visits at this stage imply that most parents make their decisions around this time, but the project's survey data clearly demonstrated that the vast majority of parents decided which school they wanted more than a year before (see Chapter 5). Of course, proximity and having older children already at a secondary school will influence many parents well before transfer, but it would also seem worth considering the role of the primary school and its staff, since this is the parents' and children's main contact with education prior to secondary school.

There appear to be three distinct areas where this influence could operate: (a) informally and possibly unconsciously as an implicit attitude towards a particular secondary school over a long period of time; (b) specifically at an organized parents' evening when the primary head might brief all the top-year parents about the forthcoming transfer process; and (c) intentionally or otherwise at parent–teacher interviews during the run-up to expressing a preference. The project initially concentrated its resources upon the secondary sector and attended no parents' meetings or interviews run by primary schools. However, 41 primary headteachers were interviewed about their views and roles in parental choice and all LEAs were asked about their attitude to the role of primary schools in guiding parents. The resulting picture is neither representative nor particularly uniform but it does shed some light on current practices.

For the majority of primary schools, known affiliations through catchment areas or sheer proximity already seem to exist and for many parents the child's stay at primary school will be part of a known and constantly reinforced educational itinerary towards employment or further education at 16 years or older. To some extent, for a parent to select other than the affiliated school or schools is to break this mould. This influence was particularly noticeable in the Roman Catholic schools we talked with where there was an expectation that parents would stay within the Roman Catholic system.

A number of schools however broke this expected mould themselves. In two of the authorities we studied the 11+ was optional: in one case only a very small percentage of either sex would 'pass' whereas in the other case only approximately 10 per cent of girls might 'pass', there being only girls' grammar schools available. (To 'pass' and to 'get in' are taken here as being synonymous.) The secondary schools suspected individual primary schools of biasing both the entry rate and the pass rate and to a large extent their views were confirmed by subsequent primary school interviews and the parents' questionnaire responses. Most notable was one primary school which manipulated the authority's rules with respect to taking practice 11+ tests, by giving its pupils more practice tests than the authority had specified. Effectively it coached its pupils to greater 11+ success than was achieved by pupils in other schools where the authority's rules were adhered to. Word has spread and there is now pressure to get into this primary school because of its higher pass rate. It is reasonable to suppose that those prepared to move house or to drive their children some distance will reinforce the current pattern.

Not far from this primary school was another where the head did not believe in selective education. The nature of the schools' two catchment areas was such that in this second school one might expect a lower 11+ pass rate, but even so the grammar school suspected this school of having a particularly low entry and pass rate. Few parents from this school reported their child as having taken the 11+ and a number commented that if they wanted 11+ advice the head was the last person to go to. Here also, one might expect the LEA's coaching rules to be more than rigidly adhered to.

In a different LEA we encountered a primary school where a significant proportion of its leavers went to a secondary school in a different town. No other children in the primary school's home town made this move and furthermore these parents had to pay significant costs for transport. It seems fair to attribute this influence on the parents and children to the primary school.

These three instances all describe decisions that have to be made before the local school 'choice' procedures come into effect and quite where attitudes, influence and information merge is difficult to determine. Certainly influence is being exerted, but this is not necessarily a negative feature, since it is also being exerted when the approved, affiliated or pyramid school is encouraged.

In a number of authorities the potential for primary schools to help with administrative formalities and to influence or guide parents has been recognized, and in some cases formalized. Several LEAs ask their primary heads to hold parents' meetings to explain the admissions procedures and to help parents use the system fully, and in at least one authority the parents' application forms are actually filled in by the primary head during an interview with the parents.

Many LEAs are nevertheless very wary of the kind of advice heads can offer and draw a sharp distinction between procedural advice and discussions on the merits or otherwise of individual secondary schools. It seems that from time to time parents have come before appeals committees and used the primary head's comments as evidence to support their case. Thus the primary head, perhaps unwittingly, can put the LEA in a difficult position, although for the most part one would assume the head's advice to be of a very different form to the LEA's defence of its position in an appeal (see Chapter 7). It is because primary heads are in such a pivotal position for offering advice, since ideally they should know something about all the immediate secondary schools and also know a good deal about the child's needs, that the project followed this line of inquiry and asked all LEAs about their expected roles for primary heads. The LEAs' responses are given in Table 4.2.

The distinction between procedural and educational advice is clearly evident in that virtually 60 per cent of respondents wanted only procedural advice to be given. Interestingly, a number of those who replied in this way took a different stance regarding the giving of specific types of advice. They were asked, for instance, whether primary heads should advise the parents of a child in need of remedial help to choose a local school, where perhaps there was little emphasis on special needs, or an alternative school with a

Table 4.2: **What is the expected role of primary heads when discussing secondary schools with parents?**

Response	catchment area		'free choice' area		all areas	
	N	%	N	%	N	%
(a) We have not advised primary heads on this	11	14	2	4	13	10
(b) We ask primary heads to use their discretion	7	9	3	6	10	8
(c) We have asked primary heads to help parents understand the system but *not* to comment on the merits or otherwise of individual schools	40	53	34	70	74	59
(d) We welcome any guidance that the primary heads can offer	10	13	8	16	18	14
(e) Other	2	3	1	2	3	2
(f) Missing	6	8	1	2	7	6
TOTAL	76	100%	49	100%	125	99%

particularly strong special needs department. Many of the officers thought that in this case the parents should be encouraged to consider the alternative school. The demarcation between 'procedural' and 'educational' advice is perhaps, therefore, not very clear.

The position of primary heads is obviously a sensitive issue and it is noticeably more so in free choice areas than in catchment areas. It seems as if in some free choice areas parents must not be advised on educational issues by the primary heads who should be more or less disinterested parties in this process. In one LEA we were shown an authority memorandum to the heads specifically stating that they must not discriminate between schools in their advice to parents.

Some authorities however adopted a different approach and seemed able to tackle this issue head on. In one LEA primary heads received a long letter describing the admissions procedures and suggesting the type of advice the heads might properly give. The authority suggested to the heads that:

> Parents are encouraged to look to you for advice and guidance and they should be offered the opportunity of personal interviews to discuss their child's future education. THE RESPONSIBILITY FOR OFFERING ADVICE RESTS WITH YOU and must not be left solely to class teachers. It is important that your advice and that of the class teachers should not be at variance.

Having clearly given the primary heads a good deal of responsibility, the authority seemed then to lose its purpose and its subsequent procedural and educational advice became intertwined. The authority continued:

> Parents should also be advised against giving any of 1983's over-subscribed schools as 2nd or 3rd preference as it is very likely that these schools will be over-subscribed once again. Will you please check each (preference) form very carefully and if, in your opinion, an unwise preference has been expressed, you should ask the parents to see you personally and advise them of the problems of their expressed preference . . . It is essential that Head Teachers offer good advice to parents expressing poor preference . . . As a general rule the school which parents should be advised to choose is the appropriate school nearest to their home or where an older brother or sister will be attending next year. Every effort should be made to encourage the idea of 'parity of esteem' among the secondary schools and to dispel the idea that there are 'superior' and 'inferior' schools.

This authority operated a free choice system and stated elsewhere that: 'The main criterion will continue to be parental preference which will be met wherever possible'. Furthermore they required primary heads to participate in the procedures and to advise parents, and they required all their secondary schools to hold open evenings, the dates of which were published by the LEA. In the end, however, they reverted to this line of 'parity of esteem' and suggested that proximity between home and school should be one of the most important factors – a move that virtually contradicted their other procedures.

Perhaps this example best demonstrates the ambiguity in the primary schools' role of informing and helping parents to choose. For several years as the child progresses through primary school, the parents will have been encouraged to turn to the primary stall for educational advice. Then, at a time when the primary head could be in the best position to advise, the authorities tend to lose confidence. It would seem that choice of secondary school can in some LEAs be best dealt with by using the distance criterion, whilst in other authorities it is too sensitive and important for primary schools to become significantly involved in.

Conclusion

The purpose of this chapter has been to consider the provision of information for parental choice beyond the legal minimum. It should not be forgotten, however, that a number of LEAs failed to satisfy this minimum, and a further few presented some of their information sufficiently ambiguously for it potentially to diminish the parents' access to the system.

At the beginning of this chapter three questions were posed:

(1)   Are parents well served by the current levels of provision?

(2)   Does the school use the provision of information constructively to gain any other benefits that might accrue?

(3)   Is the nature of the information and its provision being used to influence the degree of involvement in the choice of school?

The answer to the first question about the adequacy of the information provided inevitably seems to have reflected the amount of choice available. In catchment-area authorities the distribution of information tended to be highly localized, and individual initiatives by schools were frowned upon. Open evenings were not particularly common. In free choice areas we saw many attempts to present a unified view of schools in the brochures, though there were more open evenings. Rarely did we see the written information meeting the challenge of allowing parents to make considered, informed choices between schools. As for encouraging informed choice to improve schools, in only a few instances was the written information provided near to being adequate for this sort of demand. Of the various types of information provided, the open evening or daytime visit seemed the most informative (see also Elliott *et al.*, 1981) and it is a pity that so many schools do not hold them.

With reference to the second question of whether open evenings, school brochures and the act of choosing are seen by schools as a means of increasing parent and pupil commitment and involvement, then many schools and authorities failed to make full use of the 1980 Act legislation to gain this important spin-off.

With respect to the third question, there was clear evidence of the information being used to reinforce LEA policy. The less choice that was available, the less school information was provided. Cynically, it might be said that this was done to avoid misleading the parents, but equally it would be fair to say that a number of LEAs strove to economize on printing costs and tried not to raise parents' expectations unduly.

Whilst all of what has been described so far might suggest a degree of coherence in the LEAs' policies for the provision of information, in practice much of what we observed was simply the continuation of earlier, pre-1982 procedures with some acknowledgement to the 1980 Act. There were few examples of LEAs which had consciously thought out the complete package of information, and when we asked the education officers whether they knew if the LEA and school brochures provided the information parents wanted, not one had an answer better than that they had received no complaints; but there again, the implementation of the 1980 Act is still in its infancy. Overall there was a sort of 'information complacency' that was reinforced by financial constraints, and from this study it would be difficult to conclude that the 1980 Act had brought about the publication of enough information to allow informed choice.

CHAPTER 5

The Parents' Responses: Family Circumstances and LEA Practice

Part of the project's remit was to study parents' perceptions of, and responses to, 'choosing' their children's secondary schools. This was achieved by the use of interviews and self-completion questionnaires in the four case-study LEAs where the educational and historical contexts were already well known to the project. Since the responses to any inquiry are very much dependent upon the way the questions are asked, this chapter starts by describing how the research was conducted. The parents' responses to these questions are then considered in terms of their own employment and education, before the focus narrows down on to the specific effects of the individual LEA practice. In many ways this chapter is a prelude to Chapter 6 where we consider the impact on the parents of the individual schools in these case study LEAs.

The Parents' Questionnaire and Sample

The research was faced with three problems: (a) parents might be expected primarily to react to local rather than national contexts; (b) in many areas it was likely that only a small percentage of parents would choose a school anyway, and (c) involvement in 'choice' procedures was thought by many teachers and education officers to be related to social class, and thus it was argued that those who did not participate in choosing a school would also be unlikely to return a questionnaire. A sampling framework was chosen which could meet all these problems as well as being fairly economical. It could not, however, be nationally representative. The sample was to comprise the parents of pupils who had just transferred to any of the 14 case-study secondary schools in three of the authorities where the project was already working. In the fourth authority the sample would comprise the parents of the final-year pupils in 22 primary schools which were local to the project's four case-study secondary schools in that authority. The admissions procedures in these four authorities were well known to the researchers and work had already commenced on interviewing the primary and secondary heads and on visiting the schools (see Table 5.12 for a brief description of these authorities). The questionnaire was designed to produce responses which could be analysed in terms of known school and LEA contexts. Furthermore, as the numbers would be large, approximately 3300, and whole transfer populations could be used in two of the four areas, with two-thirds and one-third populations in the other two LEAs, the data should be able to cope with low rates of involvement and class differences if either were found to be operative.

By giving a questionnaire to the parents of pupils admitted to specific secondary schools the project had to ask what had happened to those parents who had wanted other schools and whose children had successfully gained places in them. It was possible that the sample was thereby biased. In terms of the 1980 Act a school has three types of pupil on its roll, and two types missing:

1   local pupils who wanted to get in and were successful;
2   distant pupils who wanted to get in and were successful;
3   local pupils who wanted other schools but were unsuccessful;
4   (missing) distant pupils who wanted to get in but were unsuccessful;
5   (missing) local pupils who wanted other schools and were successful.

If the project had used individual schools and ignored the others in the vicinity, it would have lost the parents of the 'missing' children, i.e. the fourth and fifth groups. However in two of the four areas, Shiretown and Northtown, the project was working with all the schools in the vicinity and could thus 'pick up' most of the parents in whichever school their child gained a place. This was also likely to occur in the third area, Seatown, where most of the schools were involved and geographic barriers, i.e. a river and the railway, helped contain the sample. In the fourth authority, London borough of Southborough, this could not be the case as the amount of 'choice' and number of schools available were too large. In this instance therefore, it was decided to approach the parents after the allocation procedures had been settled, but whilst their children were still at the primary school. Twenty-two of this authority's 89 primary schools were chosen for this sample on the basis of their being the 'main' contributory schools for the project's four case study secondary schools in this area. It was recognized, however, that many of these parents would opt away from the four schools since this was an optimal choice authority with no obvious 'linking'. These 22 primary schools had approximately one-third of the authority's transfer cohort on their rolls.

The parents were thus surveyed in two groups: one group of primary parents were approached during the summer term of their child's last year at primary school in one LEA, and a larger group of secondary parents were approached one week into their child's first term in secondary school in three other LEAs. All the information gained relates to transfer to secondary school over the summer of 1984.

Since all the parents in the survey were chosen because their children attended a small number of known schools, the project asked the schools if they would distribute and collect the questionnaires on its behalf. This was done most willingly and it is felt that the school connection enhanced the final high response rates which are shown in Table 5.1.

This response rate has also been attributed to the relevance of the questions. During the autumn and spring terms of 1983/84 the researchers interviewed a number of parents whose children had transferred in September 1983 to the same schools as were later used in the final sample. The interview schedules were developed into pilot forms of the questionnaire and these were tried out in nearby schools, again with the parents of children who transferred in 1983. The pilot sample amounted to approximately 20 per cent of the final sample size. Comments were also invited from heads, teachers, LEA officers and the project's steering committee and all the information was brought together to produce the final versions of the questionnaire.

Table 5.1:   Parents' questionnaire response summary

	Southborough LEA (Primary)	Shiretown LEA (Secondary)	Seatown LEA (Secondary)	Northtown LEA (Secondary)	Total
Number of transfer pupils on roll at time of survey	937	965	811	598	3311
Number of completed, returned question- naires	641	822	735	542	2740
Successful response rate	68.4%	85.2%	90.6%	90.6%	82.8%

It had been intended to put the same questions to all the parents in the sample. However, in order to maintain localized relevance a number of small changes had to be made. The main version of the questionnaire was used in the two selective areas, Seatown and Northtown (see Appendix 3.1). In the one fully comprehensive area, Shiretown, the 11+ questions were deleted, and in Southborough, which had selection for girls only (to two voluntary-aided schools), the 11+ questions were rephrased accordingly. In this same authority, Southborough, as the pupils were still in the primary school at the time of the survey, the verb tenses were changed where necessary to reflect that the child had yet to move to the secondary school although school places and acceptances had already been sorted out for virtually 98 per cent of the sample.

The questionnaire was written to be filled in once for each transferring child; it was assumed that one or both parents could give a single, 'family' response for details about choice. However, separate information about employment and education was sought for each parent. The questionnaire covered the issues of talking about, reading about, visiting and choosing a school, as well as issues concerning the child, the primary school and the parents themselves. Because of the project's involvement in the four LEA areas it was already possible to provide the contexts to the parents' responses and to compare their perceptions with what was known to happen. However, to be certain of a correct understanding, the project returned after the survey to three of the four LEAs, and to several of the schools, to discuss the parents' overall responses. This exercise revealed a number of instances where the schools and their authorities disagreed about the procedures being used although, for the most part, the parents', schools' and LEAs' accounts tallied well.

The Parents and the Influences of Family Circumstances

The project received information concerning 2740 transferring children of whom 52.1 per cent were girls. As all four authorities operated transfer at 11, it may be assumed that the children had an average age of about 11½ years at that time. Of these children, 55.6 per cent had older siblings, a figure that drops in the grammar schools to about 50 per cent, but that otherwise remains constant across the sample. Rephrased, this means that some 44 per cent of the parents were encountering secondary school allocation for the first time since they themselves were at school.

It would be wrong, however, to assume that all these parents were necessarily 'new' to education, since across the whole sample 19 per cent of the mothers and 9 per cent of fathers held jobs which brought them into contact with schools and teachers. Furthermore, as over half the parents knew their child's primary school teachers 'quite well' or 'very well' (Table 5.2) it may be assumed that many had been involved with their child's primary schooling. The parents' experience of local issues might be further reinforced since the sample appeared to be fairly stable with just over 93 per cent of the pupils reported as being at their most recent primary school for at least a year or more, a figure that was consistent across the four authorities.

Table 5.2:   Parents' responses to:
How well did you know any of your child's primary school teachers?

. . . *knew them by name only*	:	10.3%
. . . *knew them to say hello to*	:	21.6%
. . . *knew them quite well*	:	42.8%
. . . *knew them very well*	:	19.7%
not answered	:	5.6%

Total 2740 parents   =   100%

The Six Family Measures

Looking at the parents' responses to the other questions in the survey, many differences occur depending upon the way the sample is grouped, and it is the analysis of these differences that allows insight into the process of choice. Because of the way the sample and questionnaire were structured it is possible to consider the differences in the parents' responses in terms of: (a) various family features; (b) varying LEA procedures; and (c) the individual schools within the LEA. In focusing on the family features the questionnaire sought information on six 'family' measures which were thought might influence how the parents went about 'choosing' a school. The six measures were:

1   the child's sex;
2   whether the child had elder siblings;
3   the terminal-education* age of the mother;
4   the terminal-education* age of the father;
5   the mother's job;
6   the father's job.

The first four of these are relatively straightforward questions to ask. Seeking information about people's jobs is more sensitive and losses occurred both where a number of parents failed to answer the question, and later, where not all the descriptions could be classified because insufficient or ambiguous descriptions were

---

* Terminal-education age is the age at which the individual stopped receiving full-time continuous education.

sometimes provided. The project asked the following question of each parent, i.e. for both mothers and fathers: *'Please give a brief outline of your present or most recent job, describing what you do and mentioning any responsibilities, necessary qualifications, the size of the organization and whether you are self employed.'*

Using the National Readership Survey Classification (Monk, 1978) the parents' classifiable jobs were graded on a 1–6 scale where 1 represented the very good, top managerial and professional jobs, and 6 represented unskilled labouring. As 'housewife' could not be placed on this 1–6 scale it was classified as 7, and 8, 9 and 0 represented other forms of answers, i.e. respectively: left home, indecipherable, and part-time job of such a small nature that it may be considered as irrelevant in the terms of 1–6, e.g. working at an Oxfam shop one afternoon per week. On the basis of the 1–6 gradings alone the project was usefully able to classify 48 per cent of mothers' and 77 per cent of fathers' jobs: most of the difference between the two being accounted for by the 29 per cent of mothers who recorded their job as being a housewife. The full distributions are shown in Table 5.3.

Table 5.3: Distribution of classified responses to employment questions*

Job Classification		Mothers' Jobs		Fathers' Jobs	
NRS†	IPC	N	%	N	%
A	(1)	8	0.3	56	2.0
B	(2)	104	3.8	471	17.2
C_1	(3)	784	28.6	704	25.7
C_2	(4)	88	3.2	575	21.0
D	(5)	327	11.9	245	8.9
E	(6)	12	0.4	66	2.4
(cumulative sub-total)		(1323)	(48.3)	(2117)	(77.3)
	(7) housewife	784	28.6	1	0.0
	all other	181	6.6	198	7.2
	missing	452	16.5	424	15.5
TOTAL NUMBER		2740	99.9%	2740	99.9%

* Significance testing has not in general been applied to the questionnaire data since the respondents represented a large fraction, i.e. two-thirds, of the population under study.
† National Readership Survey Classification (Monk, 1978).

The terminal-education age was also sought as it was thought to act as a parallel measure to the employment classifications (Monk, 1978) as well as being easier to collect objectively from self-completion questionnaires. The parents were asked at what age they had left school and if they had followed this immediately with any full-time course. If they had, they were asked to give the age at which they had finished full-time education. The terminal-education age is taken as being the age the parent finished full-time, continuous education. The distributions for the mothers' and fathers' terminal-education ages are given in Table 5.4, and the correlations between the four measures, employment and terminal-education age for mothers and fathers, are shown in Table 5.5.

Table 5.4:   The distributions of terminal-education ages for mothers and fathers

	Mothers		Fathers	
Age Range	Frequency	%	Frequency	%
Under 15 years	84	3.1	134	4.9
15	1010	36.9	906	33.1
16	601	21.9	481	17.6
17	260	9.5	197	7.2
18	220	8.0	190	6.9
19–20	136	5.0	117	4.3
21+	253	9.2	351	12.8
Missing	176	6.4	364	13.3
TOTAL	2740	100.0	2740	100.1

With the information on all six measures available it is possible to consider whether any of them influenced the parents' behaviour in choosing a school. Since much of the questionnaire data is thematic, an idea of this picture can be gained by looking at just certain variables which reflect, in the following order:

1 the primary school involvement;
2 the amount of information the parents used;
3 the parents' reason for choosing a school;
4 the ease of access to the school chosen; and
5 whether the parents felt they had been offered a choice.

Table 5.5: The correlations between the parents' terminal-education ages and their classified jobs

Terminal Ed. Age: Mother	–			
Terminal Ed. Age: Father	0.57	–		
#Job: Mother	0.45	0.35	–	
#Job: Father	0.45	0.52	0.46	–

All correlations significant at $p<0.001$ or better.

#Job classifications 1–6 only
scoring reversed to remove minus sign.

The Influence of the Child's Sex

The parents of both boys and girls seemed to know the primary teachers to a similar extent – see Table 5.6. However, the girls' parents, on average, visited slightly more secondary schools and saw slightly more school brochures and examination results than did the boys' parents. The average degree of satisfaction reported on each of these variables did not effectively differ between the parents of boys and the parents of girls (Table 5.7).

To investigate what was important to parents when choosing a school they were asked: '*What things were most important to you when choosing a school? Please write down no more than five points.*'

A full list of the classified reasons with the percentage of parents giving each is shown in Appendix: Table 5.1. In respect of sex differences, although several minor fluctuations were evident, no substantial differences between boys' and girls' parents' reasons were shown. Indeed, for the most part the similarities in response rate were quite remarkable.

Table 5.6:   The influence of the child's sex and position in the family on the information used

	Average 'score' of parents' knowledge of P.S. Teacher		Average no. of schools visited		Average no. of brochures read		Average no. of school exam results seen	
		N		N		N		N
Parents of . . .								
Boys	2.7	1256	0.73	1228	0.82	1117	0.70	1213
Girls	2.7	1329	0.77	1363	0.88	1387	0.76	1363
First child	2.8	1180	0.83	1152	0.99	1174	0.8	1161
Non-first child	2.7	1485	0.68	1463	0.73	1467	0.64	1437
All parents	2.76	2665	0.75	2615	0.85	2641	0.73	2598
Missing		75		125		99		142
TOTAL		2740		2740		2740		2740

As to the schools finally chosen by the parents, 64 per cent (1721) of all parents said their child would be going or goes to the secondary school nearest to where they lived. However, it seems that 66 per cent (846) of boys went to the nearest school compared with 61 per cent (875) of girls, though part of this difference may be due to the fact that the sample included a small girls' county grammar school, which might have encouraged more distant travel. There was no equivalent boys' school in the sample.

The final consideration here relates to whether parents felt they had been offered a choice of school. Whilst the differences between the response rates in different LEAs are enormous (see page 110), across the whole sample 53.8 per cent (1456) of the parents reported that they felt they had been offered a choice, compared with 39.7 per cent (1073) who said 'No'. The sex of the child made little difference to these figures.

The Influence of the Child's Position in the Family

Parents were asked whether their transferring child had any older brothers or sisters and it seems that just over half (56 per cent) were *not* first or only children. Since LEAs place so much emphasis on younger children being able to follow their elder siblings (see Chapter 3, page 41) it seemed worthwhile investigating whether this factor influenced the five variables being used to describe the parents' behaviour in choosing a school.

In general parents whose first, or only, child was transferring, knew the primary teachers very slightly better than parents of younger siblings: see Table 5.6. The first-child parents also visited more secondary schools than non-first-child parents though, as might be expected, fewer of them had visited the actual school to which their child was finally admitted (48 per cent of first-child parents compared with 57 per cent of other parent). Finally, the

Table 5.7: Parents' average 'scores' for the effectiveness of the information used by sex of child and its position in the family

	Average score# for usefulness of school visits		Average score# for usefulness of brochures		Average score# for usefulness of school exam results	
		N		N		N
Parents of . . .						
Boys	1.65	581	1.79	659	1.85	512
Girls	1.69	644	1.79	763	1.85	601
First child	1.58	539	1.73	693	1.76	518
Non-first child	1.75	692	1.85	739	1.92	601
All parents	1.67	1237	1.79	1439	1.85	1126
Missing		1503		1301		1614
TOTAL		2740		2740		2740

The higher the score (1–3) the poorer the usefulness. Thus from the 'All parents' line it can be seen that school visits are perceived as being more useful than brochure or exam results. These figures are based on the actual number of responses made to each question. If the responses are filtered to allow answers from only those who have attended one or more visits, seen one or more brochures and so on, this trend becomes more apparent.

Average value for: visits = 1.62 N = 1049
                    talks = 1.74 N = 1155
                    brochures = 1.78 N = 1286
                    exam results = 1.81 N = 937

In other words, school visits are the most appreciated whereas exam results are the least though the differences are not particularly large.

parents of first or only children saw both more brochures and more examination results than the non-first-child parents and they also found them marginally more useful (Table 5.7).

The Influence of the Parents' Education and Jobs

The influence of the parents' jobs and terminal-education ages upon their contact with the primary school teachers and the amounts of information they used can be seen in Tables 5.8 and 5.9. There are fairly clear trends in these tables that show that the better the parents' jobs or education, the better they knew their child's primary teachers and the more information they used.

However these trends are not uniform across all the types of information. Thus although on average, the mothers with category 1 job descriptions (the 'better' jobs) saw over seven times as many examination results as their category 6 counterparts with the 'poorer' jobs (Table 5.9A), this scale of difference was not to be found with all types of information. Furthermore, within any one category of parents there was a differential take-up of information; for instance, the category 6 parents saw roughly three times more brochures than examination results. This variation in the rate of take-up of the different types of information within the same category of parents was also seen, but to a lesser extent, with the group 1 parents. It may be that the restriction in range here occurred because these parents had effectively reached a ceiling for the availability of the materials and schools: their potential take-up was being limited by the number of schools and amounts of information available.

Surprisingly, when the parents were asked about the usefulness of the visits, brochures and exam results, no trends with respect to their employment or education were visible but then these results only applied to those who used the information (see Table 5.7 for average values). The differences that existed here were in the take-up of the information and not in the value stated by those who used it.

In listing the things that were most important to them when choosing schools, 2245 parents responded to give 7689 classifiable reasons between them, an average of 3.4 reasons per responding family (see Appendix: Table 5.1). The reasons were classified into

Table 5.8: The parents' average 'scores' for how well they knew any of their child's primary school teachers by (A) jobs, and (B) terminal-education ages

A: Jobs

Job Classification		Mothers' mean 'score'#	Mothers N	Fathers' mean 'score'#	Fathers N
A	(1)	2.6	8	2.8	55
B	(2)	3.0	101	3.0	465
C_1	(3)	2.9	771	2.8	689
C_2	(4)	2.8	86	2.7	571
D	(5)	2.6	325	2.6	243
E	(6)	2.7	12	2.3	66
missing		–	1437	–	651
TOTAL		–	2740	–	2740

B: Terminal-Education Ages

Terminal Ed. Age	Mothers' mean 'score'#	Mothers N	Fathers' mean 'score'#	Fathers N
up to 15 years	2.6	82	2.7	133
15	2.6	998	2.7	896
16	2.8	594	2.8	473
17	2.8	256	2.8	194
18	3.0	216	2.8	187
19+20	2.8	132	2.8	116
21	3.0	248	2.9	342
missing	–	214	–	399
TOTAL (all ages)		2740		2740

#The higher the 'score' (1–4), the better the parents knew the primary teachers.

97 groups. With so many groups any analysis incorporating the parents' employment and education is virtually impossible. However, one way of looking at the data derives from Elliott's work which reorganizes the reasons on a process or product basis (Elliott *et al.*, 1981). Process reasons are those which relate to how the

school works, i.e. its banding system or discipline and so forth. Product reasons look to the end product, for example the school's examination success and university entrance rates. Elliott argued that some parents were process oriented whereas others looked to the products. The 97 categories in the original classification were thus regrouped as: (A) process; (B) product; (C) geographic; and, (D) unclassifiable. Geography, i.e. distance from home to school, was added since it appeared to form the basis of a separate yet homogeneous group. (The regrouping label, A, B, C or D, for each of the 97 reasons is shown in Appendix: Table 5.1.)

The analysis of process, product and geographic reasons, by the parents' education, showed that as the length of the parents' education increased, there was a very slight trend for the proportion of geographic reasons to reduce, with most of this reduction being accounted for by increases in the numbers of process reasons.

Table 5.9: The influence of (A) the parents' jobs, and (B) the parents' terminal-education age on the information used by parents before choice

A: Jobs		Average no. of visits made		Average no. of brochures seen		Average no. of exam results seen	
Mothers' Job		%	N	%	N	%	N
A	(1)	2.2	6	1.5	8	1.5	8
B	(2)	1.9	67	1.3	103	1.4	103
C$_1$	(3)	1.6	435	1.0	770	1.0	758
C$_2$	(4)	1.6	43	0.8	86	0.7	87
D	(5)	1.3	120	0.7	316	0.5	309
E	(6)	1.0	2	0.7	12	0.2	12
Missing		–	2067	–	1445	–	1463
TOTAL		–	2740	–	2740	–	2740
Fathers' Job							
A	(1)	2.0	40	1.2	56	1.1	55
B	(2)	1.7	278	1.1	464	1.2	462
C$_1$	(3)	1.5	352	0.9	688	0.8	683
C$_2$	(4)	1.5	231	0.7	561	0.5	548
D	(5)	1.4	104	0.7	234	0.5	231
E	(6)	1.3	16	0.5	66	0.2	64
Missing		–	1719	–	671	–	697
TOTAL		–	2740	–	2740	–	2740

Table 5.9 cont.

B: Terminal-Education Ages

Mothers' Terminal-Education Age

	%	N	%	N	%	N
up to 15 years	1.4	31	0.6	82	0.4	82
15	1.3	396	0.7	981	0.5	956
16	1.5	294	0.8	585	0.7	581
17	1.7	122	0.9	256	1.0	248
18	1.6	118	1.0	218	0.9	217
19+20	1.7	83	1.1	135	1.1	136
21+	2.0	158	1.4	245	1.4	241
Missing	–	1538	–	238	–	279
TOTAL	–	2740	–	2740	–	2740

Fathers' Terminal-Education Age

	%	N	%	N	%	N
up to 15 years	1.5	64	0.8	130	0.6	131
15	1.3	364	0.7	877	0.5	855
16	1.5	230	0.8	466	0.8	462
17	1.5	109	0.9	192	0.9	193
18	1.7	94	1.0	187	1.1	184
19+20	1.8	58	0.9	117	0.7	114
21+	1.8	215	1.2	346	1.2	341
Missing	–	1606	–	425	–	460
TOTAL	–	2740	–	2740	–	2740

Basically, however, the proportions at 68 per cent process, 18 per cent product and 14 per cent geography were stable against terminal-education ages and the sex of parent. A very similar pattern was found in the analyses which looked at the influences of the parents' job descriptions on the reasons they gave. The same cannot be said about the absolute numbers of reasons given since these increased with both these measures. Where parents gave several reasons the distribution of the different types became of interest and it is striking that only a very small percentage of parents gave product only, or product and geography only reasons. Seen from the other perspective approximately 90 per cent of parents included process reasons in what they considered important when choosing a school, whereas only just over half the parents (54 per cent) gave any product reasons at all. (See Appendix 3.1 for how to obtain details of this analysis.)

The final two variables to consider in this section relate to the outcomes of participating in choosing a school, i.e. did the parents' jobs and education influence their answers to the questions of whether the school chosen was nearest to home, and whether parents felt they had been offered a choice? The answers to these two questions both showed the parents' education and jobs to influence the outcome. On the basis of the father's job, the likelihood of the child going to the nearest secondary school decreased from 77 per cent for fathers with category 6 jobs, to 38 per cent for category 1 fathers – a trend that is maintained with the mother's employment and both parents' education (see Table 5.10).

Tables 5.10 and 5.11:   Influence of parents' education and jobs on the nearness of the secondary school the child goes to and whether they felt they were offered a choice

		Table 5.10 Is the school your child goes to the nearest where you live?			**Table 5.11** Do you feel you were offered a choice of school?		
		Yes%	No%	N	Yes%	No%	N
Mothers' Job	1	(37.5)	(62.5)	8	(100.0)	(0.0)	7
	2	53.4	46.6	103	52.0	48.0	102
	3	56.9	43.1	777	52.8	47.2	755
	4	57.5	42.5	87	68.7	31.3	83
	5	72.3	27.7	325	59.1	40.9	301
	6	(58.3)	(41.7)	12	(40.0)	(60.0)	10
Missing				1428			1482
TOTAL				2740			2740
Fathers' Job	1	38.2	61.8	55	78.2	21.8	55
	2	53.2	46.8	468	50.4	49.6	458
	3	59.5	40.5	698	53.4	46.6	671
	4	68.0	32.0	572	61.1	38.9	537
	5	74.8	25.2	242	70.4	29.6	226
	6	77.3	22.7	66	80.3	19.7	61
Missing				639			732
TOTAL				2740			2740

	Table 5.10 (contd)			Table 5.11 (contd)		
Mothers' Terminal-Education Age (years)						
	Yes%	No%	N	Yes%	No%	N
up to 15	73.5	26.5	83	75.6	24.4	78
15	72.6	27.4	1007	57.6	42.4	934
16	61.3	38.7	600	57.2	42.8	570
17	56.9	43.1	253	52.5	47.5	244
18	60.1	39.9	218	55.3	44.7	208
19+20	57.0	43.0	135	60.8	39.2	130
21+	45.6	54.4	250	59.0	41.0	244
Missing			194			332
TOTAL			2740			2740

Fathers' Terminal-Education Age (years)						
up to 15	69.9	30.1	133	69.9	30.1	123
15	71.3	28.7	899	58.0	42.0	841
16	64.4	35.6	481	53.4	46.6	453
17	58.2	41.8	196	52.9	47.1	191
18	57.1	42.9	189	52.2	47.8	182
19+20	55.7	44.3	115	56.6	43.4	113
21+	49.4	50.6	344	58.9	41.1	341
Missing			383			496
TOTAL			2740			2740

The question of whether parents felt they had been offered a choice of school is influenced in a different way, with those with extreme scores for education and employment feeling that there was more choice than did those in the middle ranges of education and employment. These differences were considerable (see Table 5.11).

Family Influences in Perspective

This section investigated how much 'family' matters influenced how the parents set about choosing a school. Six measures were looked at: the child's sex and position in the family, and the mothers' and fathers' individual job categories and their respective terminal-education ages. The 'choice' variables used were the degree of involvement with the primary school, the amounts of information used, the reasons given for choosing a school, the distance between home and the chosen school, and whether the parents felt they had been offered a choice.

Neither the sex of the child nor its position in the family seemed to exert much influence although the parents of girls and first children reported using marginally more information than other parents. Interestingly the girls' parents found the information no more useful than boys' parents. Parents of first children appeared slightly more likely than other parents to send their children to a school which was not the nearest to their home. The child's sex made no apparent difference to perceptions of choice but parents of first children felt there to be less choice than did parents of second or subsequent children. In all, the differences were small.

This does not imply however that the child has little impact on the process. In 65.4 per cent of the responses, parents reported that their child felt strongly about the secondary school he or she was to go to. Of these 1792 parents, 77.6 per cent felt that the child's opinion was 'very important in choosing a school' and a further 20.3 per cent felt it to be 'fairly important'. The child's sex and position in the family had little impact on these figures.

The parents' own education and employment were found, however, to be more influential. The longer they were in full-time education and the higher their job classification, i.e. the nearer to being a bank manager or professor, then the more information was used and the more likely they were to choose a more distant school.

The feeling of having a choice was not so clear-cut however, with parents at the extremes of both the education and employment measures feeling there was more choice available than their counterparts in the middle ranges. Quite why this last pattern emerges is unclear, but it is conceivable that the mobility which is associated with the higher job classifications might have permitted these groups to choose the more distant schools and therefore it might have increased the feeling of choice. This argument is not supported however in Southborough, the one authority where transport was provided to *any* borough school chosen as long as it was more than three miles away. The job category 1 and category 6 parents still felt there to be more choice than the group 2 and 3 parents. It is possible, though, that three miles is too large a minimum distance to influence the travel considerations for 11-year-old children in an urban LEA.

An alternative solution to this might lie with the fact that the group 1 sample might be subject to bias since its members had the easiest access to the independent sector. This being so, one might assume that those group 1 parents who did not anticipate getting a place at the school of their choice had already left the state system and thus, by their leaving, influenced the overall group 1 response to give on average an over-positive view. This argument cannot be verified from the project's data.

LEA Influences on the Parents' Responses

The project surveyed parents in parts of four very different LEAs. Table 5.12 provides the annotated descriptions of these four areas.

Table 5.12: An annotated description of the choice procedures in the four LEA areas used by the project

AREA 1:   SHIRETOWN Comprehensive LEA emphasizing catchment areas. 26 per cent of the parents felt there was a choice of school.

Geography: Small, old county town: population of approximately 17,200.

Schools: There were nine schools in the division (see map on page 114), two of which were in Shiretown itself. The survey used four mixed comprehensives, the two from the town and two from outlying villages. The town schools were large 11–18 schools, whereas the village ones were smaller: one, an 11–16, was an active community centre, and the other was an 11–14 school with its 'upper', but separate, school nearby. No voluntary-aided schools were immediately accessible to the town for these parents.

Parents: Employment on 1–6 scale: mothers 3.5 (49%) #
                                         fathers 3.2 (76%)
              Terminal-education age: mothers 16.5 years (94%)
                                           fathers 16.9 years (88%)

Admissions Procedures:

> Catchment areas were used but a margin existed between the cohort size and the intended intake figure to allow for flexibility. Parents were initially offered reserved places in the catchment-area school and then did not have to respond unless they wanted another school.
>
> Transport was not paid for except to the catchment-area school if it was over three miles away from home address. Approximately 10 per cent of the transfer group went to a school other than their catchment-area school in 1983.

Published Criteria:

> 1   verified medical needs
> 2   sibling attendance
> 3   attendance at a linked primary school
> 4   family association
> 5   proximity and ease of access

Number of secondary appeals in division in 1984: none

Pre-choice Information:

> Brochure distribution was to catchment-area parents if at all. Only one school held pre-choice visits and then only for certain parents. Otherwise a small number of talks were held in primary schools. Exam results were distributed in the school brochures and therefore there was limited distribution.

AREA 2:   SEATOWN   Selective LEA emphasizing catchment areas. 49 per cent of the parents felt there was a choice of school.

Geography: County town with emphasis on light and electrical industries: population approximately 58,300.

Schools: Thirteen schools in the division, of which eight were in the town. Of these, five were used in the survey: one small, girls' county grammar, three mixed 'comprehensive', one mixed R.C. comprehensive. All five were 11–18 schools. One of the state comprehensive schools segregated the sexes in years 1–3 (Newcrest).

Parents: Employment on 1–6 scale: mothers 3.4 (50%)#
                                           fathers 3.2 (80%)
           Terminal-education age: mothers 16.5 years (96%)
                                     fathers 16.9 years (90%)

Admissions Procedures:

>   A   Selection: County Grammar School took 2 per cent from top 8 to 10 per cent. 11+ exam was optional and the take-up varied between primary schools.

B   Comprehensive: Clearly defined catchment areas existed with a strong expectation that children would attend their catchment-area school.

Falling rolls were managed by effecting proportional reduction in all the comprehensive schools.
Approximately 6 per cent out-catchment transfers occurred in 1983.
Transport was not paid for except to catchment-area, grammar or voluntary-aided school, if over three miles from home address.

Published Criteria:
1   sibling attendance
2   denominational
3   single-sex or co-educational wishes
4   distance from home
    (also, medical factors)

Number of secondary appeals in division in 1984: 35

Pre-choice Information:
Brochures available to catchment-area parents. School talks rather than full visits were available on request only. Exam results in 1984 were difficult to get hold of. All applicants to the Roman Catholic school were interviewed before being accepted.

AREA 3:   NORTHTOWN Selective LEA offering mixed types of choice. 66 per cent of the parents felt there was a choice of school.

Geography: Small, economically depressed northern town: population approximately 20,000.

Schools: All the secondary schools in the locality were used in the survey. These comprised:
1 mixed, small, 11–18 grammar in Northtown;
2 mixed, small, 11–16 secondary modern schools in Northtown;
1 mixed, small, 11–16 secondary modern in neighbouring agricultural village, Cattleford.
1 mixed, 11–16 comprehensive 10 miles away just into the neighbouring LEA, but part of district prior to 1974 reorganization (Riverview School).

Parents: Employment on 1–6 scale: mothers 3.9 (39%)#
                                         fathers 3.8 (77%)
                Terminal-education age: mothers 16.0 years (96%)
                                         fathers 16.0 years (88%)

Admissions Procedures:
        Selection: the 11+ exam was compulsory within grammar
        school catchment area (see map on page 137). Some
        primary schools lay in the comprehensive school catchment
        area and here the 11+ was not offered but was available on
        request. There was a small option zone for both grammar
        and comprehensive schools where parents could choose to
        enter 11+ or not. Passing the 11+ gave access to one
        grammar school only, i.e. Northtown High. Application to
        the comprehensive school, Riverview, effectively offered
        access to one comprehensive only. 11+ failure in
        Northtown gave choice between two secondary modern
        schools in the town. 11+ failure in Cattleford gave access to
        one rural secondary modern school and more recently also
        to a comprehensive school some distance away: no
        transport was provided to this last comprehensive school.
        The parents' perception of choice varied greatly from
        school to school in this LEA.

Published Criteria:
        1 denominational reasons
        2 siblings
        3 medical
        4 distance
        *(These criteria were derived by inference from the
        brochure as they were not given directly.)

Number of secondary appeals in 1984: selective 3
                                     non-selective 5

Pre-choice Information:
        For four of the five schools, brochures were available upon
        request only. A similar distribution applied for their exam
        results. The comprehensive school, Riverview, in the
        neighbouring LEA, sent brochures to its catchment-area
        parents and invited the option-zone parents to an open
        evening. There were no formally arranged talks or visits for
        the other four schools.

AREA 4: SOUTHBOROUGH A comprehensive borough with two
        selective girls' voluntary-aided schools: 84 per cent of the
        parents felt there was a choice of school.

Geography: London borough with few 'inner urban' areas: population approximately 305,000.

Schools: Twenty secondary schools including single-sex and co-educational. Most of the schools were 11–18. Eight of the schools were voluntary aided of which two were selective girls' schools. Several independent schools co-exist in the locality.

The project concentrated on four of the 11–18 mixed comprehensive schools: two were neighbouring schools with differing reputations, a third was a growing school in an area where rolls were falling, and the fourth was a popular Roman Catholic school.

Parents: Employment on 1–6 scale: mothers 3.4 (53%)#
fathers 3.2 (75%)
Terminal-education ages: mothers 17.3 years (89%)
fathers 17.7 years (80%)

Admissions Procedures:

Parents were invited to choose from all the 20 schools listed in the LEA brochure. Parents could list as many preferences as they wished and all would be treated as equal first choices. Parents were told they could not appeal against being given a place in any one of the schools they listed. Applications to the girls' grammar schools were handled within this system and the 11+ exam was taken at the grammar schools out of normal school time. Falling rolls were managed by closing or merging schools which failed to maintain a viable size. Transport was paid to *any* borough school over three miles from the home.

Criteria: Siblings and distance (priority uncertain)

Number of secondary appeals in borough in 1984: 90

Pre-choice Information:

The LEA booklet was sent to all parents and contained a full page of information about each school.
All schools held open evenings – times and dates were given in LEA booklet. School brochures were issued at open evenings and the schools' exam results were available with the brochures.

---

figures in brackets give the percentage of parents whose jobs could be classified in the range 1–6 (see page 81).

The authorities were chosen for this research to reflect both urban and rural areas, and comprehensive and selective systems: both elements thought to influence the choice available to parents. As the totally isolated rural school effectively allows no choice, small rural towns with two or more secondary schools in them were sought. Shiretown and Northtown were both suitable examples with a potential for a limited amount of choice due to the small number of schools centred in and around them. Seatown and Southborough, however, were both large enough to have schools with totally urban intakes and for there to be several schools within range of most parents' homes.

With respect to selection, the issue became far more complex than had initially been supposed. Seatown and Northtown were chosen because they had selective systems, but in Seatown only about 2 per cent of all pupils attended grammar schools whereas in Northtown this figure reached about 25 per cent. Southborough, chosen as an urban comprehensive LEA, turned out to have grammar places in voluntary-aided schools for girls only and if all these places were filled from the borough this would represent selection for approximately 13 per cent of the girls. An unknown, but not insignificant, proportion of boys in Southborough attended independent schools. Shiretown, however, seemed to be completely comprehensive. The voluntary-aided school in Seatown, a Roman Catholic mixed comprehensive, was also felt by education officers and teachers to influence choice in a mildly selective manner since it (a) required an interview prior to acceptance, (b) had a loose catchment area which covered the whole of Seatown and beyond, and (c) it accepted non-Roman Catholic children. The degree to which it acted as a third tier between the grammar and 'comprehensive' schools is difficult to determine, but the suggestion certainly existed.

The four authorities not only differed in these respects, but also, and possibly more significantly, they differed in their policies and practices for school allocation, and hence 'choice'. Shiretown parents reported *feeling* the least amount of choice of the parents in any of the four authorities; only 26 per cent of Shiretown parents felt they had been offered a choice of school, yet Shiretown rarely refused any applications for non-catchment-area schools and had no secondary appeals in 1984. Although all comprehensive, Shiretown's schools differed in various ways (see Chapter 6) and parents were likely to perceive that there was something to choose between them. Since few parents were rejected once they initiated the process of expressing a preference, one can only assume that factors such as the presentation of the system and the parents' low expectation of gaining access to their preferred school, must have contributed to this very low level of perceived choice.

In Seatown almost half the parents felt they had a choice but proportionately less out-catchment transfers took place here in 1983 than in Shiretown (Seatown, 6 per cent; Shiretown, 10 per cent). The Seatown parents, when interviewed, described the catchment-area boundaries as difficult to cross. Here, perhaps more than in Shiretown, there was a perceived hierarchy of schools with the grammar at the top, the voluntary-aided in the middle and the comprehensives, which alone were bearing the brunt of falling rolls, running third. However, as Chapter 6 indicates, there was little objective reason for such a hierarchy.

On average, 66 per cent of Northtown parents felt they had been offered a choice, but this disguises an enormous variation between the five schools, 23 per cent rising to 91 per cent. It does however demonstrate that the LEA's practice of offering a real choice between the two town secondary modern schools to these town parents whose children had not won places at the grammar school, can result in the parents feeling they were offered a choice. The quality of this choice was argued by some to debase its value. Two parents in Northtown expressed this view well:

> In the Northtown area the choice is limited. Any child who fails the 11+ must go to secondary modern schools whose level of education is far below that of the high school. Although there is the possibility of a bright child being transferred at a later age this would perhaps have adverse effects on that child.

> There really was no choice, it is just a question of crossing your fingers and hoping and thankfully breathing a big sigh of relief.

In Southborough there were no predetermined catchment areas and transport was provided to any school over three miles away – the only LEA in the four to offer this. But distance was used as an admissions criterion which effectively introduced amorphous catchment areas and denied more distant families access to popular

Table 5.13:   Parents' responses to primary school advice

*Did the primary school head
or teachers recommend one
school more than any other?*

	Area 1 Shiretown (N=822) %	Area 2 Seatown (N=735) %	Area 3 Northtown (N=542) %	Area 4 Southborough (N=641) %	Area Total (N=2740) %
YES	13.6	27.3	20.1	20.1	20.1
NO	80.7	69.3	75.8	77.5	76.0
MISSING	5.7	3.4	4.1	2.4	3.9

*Were they helpful in the
process of choosing a school?*

YES	29.9	42.2	37.8	61.9	42.2
NO	54.4	49.4	50.9	29.5	46.5
MISSING	15.7	8.4	11.3	8.6	11.3

schools. Even so, in Southborough, choice of school was a policy the authority positively promoted. Published information, therefore, was more generally available here than elsewhere and there was a coordinated policy for secondary schools to hold well-publicized open evenings. Furthermore, the continued existence of each secondary school was publicly acknowledged to depend upon its popularity: if a school could not maintain a viable roll then it would be merged or closed.

The fact that there were 90 secondary appeals in 1984 in Southborough, a figure which is proportionally more than in either Shiretown and Northtown, suggests a role for appeals which is not directly related to the amount of perceived choice. It does not seem that the less choice is offered the more parents will appeal, so much as that the more parents take up choice, then the more occasions there will be for conflict to arise, a point taken up in Chapter 7.

LEA Practice and the Primary School Involvement

Across the four LEAs the parents, on average, seemed to know their child's primary school teachers equally well (see Table 5.2).

However, they were not consistent in the degree to which they reported the involvement of the heads and teachers in making specific recommendations about individual secondary schools. Table 5.13 demonstrates the variation across the four authorities.

In Shiretown LEA, where little choice was perceived, there would be little scope for any useful recommendations and this seems borne out in practice. Seatown and Northtown both had more choice reported and had selective schools, and it would appear to be the selective schools that primarily boosted these figures, although the parents of Roman Catholic children in Seatown also received more explicit recommendations (see Chapter 6). In Southborough, where parents had more choice, the selective and Roman Catholic schools were still a significant influence on these figures. That the figures are no larger may well be due to an LEA memorandum which requested that primary school staff did not recommend any particular school. Thus there appears to be a consistent picture across the four authorities of parents being recommended to apply to grammar or Roman Catholic schools if applicable, but otherwise little emphasis being placed on the differences between comprehensive schools.

The usefulness of this primary school advice again seems to relate to the degree of choice perceived by the parents, and again, as will be seen in Chapter 6, it is the parents of children at the Roman Catholic and grammar schools who appear most appreciative. But it is possible that those parents are responding to different interpretations of the term 'choice', and that this might reflect the distinction between advice about competing for selective places and that concerning choice between like schools.

Other Sources of Information

Parents may well turn to other people for advice on choosing a school. In the questionnaire nine potential 'sources of information' were listed and parents were asked to circle those they had talked to. The results are given in Table 5.14.

The overall picture is not very clear, but features such as school visits and talks seem to have made specific impacts on the amount of secondary school contact, e.g. in Northtown LEA there were few secondary visits or talks and therefore it is understandable that only

Table 5.14: Who the parents talked to when choosing schools

Who did you talk to about the choice of school?

	Area 1 Shiretown (N=822) %	Area 2 Scatown (N=735) %	Area 3 Northtown (N=542) %	Area 4 Southborough (N=641) %	Total (N=2740) %
(1) Nobody	— 36.6	21.0	31.4	13.1	25.9
(2) Junior/Primary School Head	18.1	28.0	22.3	42.1	27.2
(3) Junior/Primary School Teachers	24.6	32.2	22.5	26.5	26.7
(4) Secondary School Head#	11.9	19.5	4.8	12.9	12.8
(5) Secondary School Teachers#	8.9	11.0	5.7	13.3	9.9
(6) Parents of children at Secondary School	36.3	46.5	26.6	41.3	38.3
(7) Other parents with 11-year-olds	24.7	32.8	20.7	28.7	27.0
(8) Your 11-year-old child	38.3	55.6	49.1	51.2	48.1
(9) Family, friends, neighbours	31.4	40.0	30.1	38.8	35.2
Average number of responses per questionnaire: *	2.35	2.89	2.13	2.55	2.51

\# The secondary school staff need not be the staff of the school the child subsequently attended.

* This figure exceeds 1 as parents were invited to tick as many responses as appropriate.

about 5 per cent of parents had spoken to either secondary heads or staff about choice. The localized effect is similarly visible in Southborough where pre-choice parents' meetings in the primary schools seem to have resulted in the large number of parents (42 per cent) who had actually spoken to the primary heads about choice.

Two other points are also visible in Table 5.14. First, in Shiretown over one-third of the parents spoke to 'nobody' ('nobody' was a

Table 5.15: The parents' use of information

A Average numbers of school visits
B Average numbers of brochures seen
C Average numbers of exam results seen, by LEA

A How many schools did you visit before you had to make your choice?	Area 1 Shiretown (N=822)	Area 2 Seatown (N=735)	Area 3 Northtown (N=542)	Area 4 Southborough (N=641)	Total (N=2740)
none %	57.2	42.7	75.3	23.6	49.0
one %	29.6	40.8	16.1	26.2	29.1
two %	4.1	10.5	4.1	22.6	10.1
three or more %	2.4	3.1	0.6	25.0	7.5
Average no. of schools visited	0.5	0.7	0.3	1.5	0.75

B How many different school brochures did you see before you had to make your choice?

no brochures %	47.6	43.3	58.3	34.2	45.4
one %	37.6	31.0	26.4	20.9	29.7
two %	6.4	17.1	8.9	17.6	12.4
three or more %	3.5	7.2	2.8	24.3	9.2
Average no. of brochures seen	0.6	0.9	0.5	1.3	0.85

C How many schools' examination results did you see before you had to make your choice?

no school's %	62.9	58.5	72.5	46.6	59.8
one %	7.9	21.8	12.0	11.9	13.4
two %	8.3	10.2	6.1	15.4	10.0
three or more %	14.6	5.6	4.6	21.8	11.9
Average no. of results seen	0.7	0.6	0.4	1.1	0.73

'positive' response on the questionnaire) and this may well relate to the minimal amount of choice that many parents perceived. Secondly just over half of all parents did not discuss the choice with their child, a somewhat surprising result considering the reported strength of the children's views.

Of course, the number of people spoken to will also be influenced by the other types of information available. Table 5.15 shows the numbers of visits made by the parents and how many brochures and examination results they saw. Again, whilst in total it is noticeable that for each type of information approximately half the parents were not actively involved, of those who were involved, the degree of involvement still varied greatly between the authorities.

Southborough LEA ensures that all its schools hold open evenings, that the dates and times are well publicized and that the invitations are borough-wide and not restricted by catchment areas. The fact that these parents make twice as many visits as the average for all four LEAs, and five times as many as Northtown parents may well be attributed to this. There is, of course, more point for the Southborough parents to visit schools because they have an actual choice to make (they have to name a school on a reply form and the LEA makes no prior 'suggestions'), though in both Shiretown and Seatown more parents visited schools than felt they had choice, which suggests that for many parents the pre-choice school visit serves other functions. Some of these reported pre-choice visits will, of course, have arisen because of the presence of older siblings already in the school. The average number of school brochures seen before choice also varied greatly from LEA to LEA. Once again Southborough parents saw the most, and almost one-quarter of them saw three or more brochures. This high proportion would seem to reflect the practice of open-evening distribution and the fact that one-quarter of Southborough's parents attended three or more open evenings.

The number of school examination results seen by parents would be expected to follow the school brochure distributions and to an extent it may be seen to do so although there is a peculiar reversal of this trend in Shiretown. However, the figures are potentially flawed. The project was aware from the earlier interviews with parents that they considered themselves as having seen school exam results when only partial versions might have been available, for instance when extracts such as scholarship and university entrance results were published in the local press. The parents were asked in the questionnaire where they saw the exam results. Table 5.16 gives the parents' responses. It is notable that in three out of the four LEAs and especially in Shiretown, few parents derived their information from the schools' brochures. In these three authorities, Shiretown, Seatown and Northtown, an average of only 11 per cent of parents saw the exam results in school brochures, i.e. in a form which the schools and LEAs could control. Where the secondary school staff gave out the 'official' school exam results this would increase the percentage of school-controlled results seen, but even so, in Shiretown, the two sources combined still only reached 10.8 per cent. In Southborough the position is very different and over half the parents reported seeing the results in school brochures.

Table 5.16: **Where parents saw the exam results**

If you saw any school examination results before you had to choose, where did you get them from?	Area 1 Shiretown (N=822)	Area 2 Seatown (N=735)	Area 3 Northtown (N=542)	Area 4 Southborough (N=641)	Total (N=2740)
	%	%	%	%	%
school brochures	7.9	14.3	11.6	54.6	21.2
secondary school staff	2.9	13.5	3.3	14.0	10.2
primary school staff	1.5	2.6	1.7	2.6	2.1
local newspapers	28.3	11.4	9.2	5.5	14.7
friends, people at work	4.6	6.4	3.0	5.7	5.0
other parents	18.3	8.6	5.0	13.6	11.9
(#No exam results reported as being seen)	69.2	62.4	77.3	50.9	64.7

This result includes the missing response.
Total percentages exceed 100 as parents were invited to tick as many responses as appropriate.

The local press can be seen as the second most popular source, and indeed, in Shiretown the local press is used three times as much as the school brochures alone and this may account for the reversal. But with the local press, the school and LEA have little say in how the results are presented. The primary school involvement in distributing exam results, or even just acting as a library of brochures and so forth, is apparently very small.

Across all four LEAs, of those parents who used any of the officially supplied information, i.e. visits, brochures and exam results, more parents found them, on average, to 'confirm their views', than to be 'most useful' or otherwise, see Table 5.17. However, this was not the case in Southborough where the largest response in each instance was that they were 'most useful'. With only four authorities it is difficult to draw conclusions, but one might hypothesize from these data that the parents found the information more useful when they had a real choice to make.

In general there appeared to be a weak trend towards the visits being seen as the most useful source of information, but as the question was not put directly, the most useful source is difficult to determine. However, when the project interviewed parents, many suggested that it would be useful if the brochures could be distributed prior to the visits so that they, the parents, could select visits on the basis of brochures. In other words these information sources can be seen as being complementary rather than competing, and as such they serve different purposes.

Table 5.17: The parents' responses regarding the usefulness of the information

If you visited one or more schools before you had to make your choice do you feel that the visits . . .		Area 1 Shiretown	Area 2 Seatown	Area 3 Northtown	Area 4 Southborough	Total
(number of parents who visited one or more schools		297	400	112	473	1282)
were most useful in choosing a school?	%	24	32	31	51	37
only confirmed what you already felt?	%	41	45	36	35	40
were of little use in choosing a school?	%	9	6	2	4	5
Not answered	%	27	17	31	11	18
TOTAL	%	101	100	100	101	100

Table 5.17 cont.

If you read one or more brochures do you feel that the brochures . . . (number of parents who read one or more brochures		Area 1 Shiretown	Area 2 Seatown	Area 3 Northtown	Area 4 Southborough	Total
		391	407	206	403	1407)
were most useful in choosing a school?	%	29	34	27	49	36
only confirmed what you already felt?	%	43	43	44	31	40
were of little use in choosing a school?	%	15	18	17	13	16
Not answered	%	13	5	12	6	9
TOTAL	%	100	100	100	99	101

If you saw any school exam results do you feel that they . . . (number of parents who saw one or more sets of exam results						
		253	276	123	315	967)
were most useful in choosing a school?	%	30	34	24	43	34
only confirmed what you already felt?	%	46	51	57	38	47
were of little use in choosing a school?	%	19	12	19	16	16
Not answered	%	4	3	1	3	3
TOTAL	%	99	100	101	100	100

Reasons for Choosing a School

In all four authorities, the parents' most commonly mentioned important factor when choosing a school was 'academic record', but having said this, Seatown parents listed it twice as often as Northtown parents: see Table 5.18. The second most frequently stated item was 'good discipline', which appears in this position for all but Southborough where it follows 'short distance', the third reason given in the other authorities. Overall, given the large

Table 5.18: The five most important reasons for choosing a school

	Area 1 Shiretown N=822	Area 2 Seatown N=735	Area 3 Northtown N=542	Area 4 Southborough N=641
Percentage of parents giving reason				
50			academic record	
45				academic record
40	academic record		good discipline	
35				short distance
30	good discipline			
25			academic record good discipline	good discipline
20		short distance	short distance	
15	short distance good reputation wide subject choice	good reputation wide subject choice		single-sexed good reputation
10			good reputation wide subject choice	
Percentage of reasons/parents	2.5	3.1	2.4	3.3

Full version of reasons

Academic record = Good standards of education/exam results/academic record.
Good discipline = Good discipline.
Short distance = Short distance/close (inc. locality = nearness)
Good reputation = Good reputation/well recommended – vague but positive.
Wide subject choice = Wide choice of subjects/options – broad curriculum.
Single-sex education = Single-sex including boys only or girls only and single-sex teaching for part of school.

differences between the amount of perceived choice and other characteristics in these four areas it is perhaps the uniformity of the parents' reasons that is most striking. However, looking at the biggest differences, Northtown parents gave fewer reasons per head than other parents but not so few as would explain why 'academic record' appears less important. Similarly, in geographical terms, since Seatown is neither twice as compact nor spread out as Southborough there must be some other reason why Southborough parents gave 'short distance' as the second most important reason as opposed to Seatown's third. It should be noted here that in giving the five most popular reasons, approximately one-and-a-half times as many reasons are being ignored in this table. (See Appendix: Table 5.1 for full list.)

The Outcome – the Chosen School

The final issue to consider is the one measure which gives some idea of the final outcome of the parents' choice. The parents were asked if the secondary school their child went to (or was due to go to in Southborough), was the nearest to where they lived. In Shiretown 71 per cent of pupils attended their nearest school. Comparable figures for Seatown, Northtown and Southborough were 59 per cent, 73 per cent and 52 per cent respectively. In the authority with most perceived choice, Southborough, more pupils attended the more distant schools. This presumably implies that with this feeling of choice almost half of the parents were rejecting their 'local' school, as did just over one-quarter of the parents in Shiretown and Northtown, although catchment-area boundaries will confound this since the catchment-area school is not always the nearest. Of course, schools that are distant for some are local for others, and thus if 48 per cent of parents choose other than the local school, we are no wiser about the specific educational advantages they may have gained. However, if by choosing a specific school the parents can feel that they have obtained a place at the school they want, then the process of choice itself may have brought about advantages.

The LEA Influence in Perspective

The project asked similar or identical questions of parents in four very different authorities where a good deal was known about the admissions procedures, schools and geography. The parents' responses to many but not all of these questions differed considerably and attempts have been made to identify the underlying causes for these differences.

The selection of these authorities has been very fortuitous in that the use of urban/rural and comprehensive/selective dimensions to identify four LEAs for further research has, by chance, resulted in the finding of LEAs where the parents' perception of choice varied from 26 per cent in Shiretown, via 49 per cent in Seatown and 66 per cent in Northtown, to 84 per cent in Southborough. Consideration of the possible influences that might cause such a wide variation, e.g. LEA policy, admissions criteria, geography, selective systems and diversity, seems to suggest two types of factor. First there is the limiting factor, for instance distance from schools. If a school is miles from any other school, then the parents cannot practically choose between two or more schools and this can limit their choice, but that is not to say that if several schools are close together then choice will automatically follow. Given that the limitations are overcome, mainly in urban situations, the second type of factor, the facilitating type, comes into play. In this instance the LEA can choose whether to encourage and facilitate choice, perhaps even to give it priority over other educational policies.

In the areas studied there were, for the most part, few limiting factors which were beyond the control of the authority, although, given the political sensitivities of 11+ selection, this may be one of them. For the majority of the parents who were sent questionnaires the degree of choice they were offered was effectively determined by the authority. That they should have perceived such different amounts of choice must be a reflection on the implementation of the 1980 Act.

However, in answering the question on their perceptions of choice, the parents were not being asked to give a factual or legalistic answer. Instead, since none of these authorities offered 'choice' per se, the parents were asked about whether they *felt* they had been offered a choice. The difference is important since technically even where choice was not available, all these parents were entitled to state a preference which would have to be accepted by the home or neighbouring authority if places were available in the preferred school. The concept of perceived choice also means that in saying yes or no, parents may have been reacting to different facets, e.g. for some the choice between a 'good' and a 'bad' school was no choice, whilst for others a marginal transport cost may have assumed great importance. The project can offer no insight into this variation except that which might be caused by the differences between schools, and this is explored in the next chapter. In terms of the provision and use of information, where the LEA offered little choice, little information accompanied it and parents did not seem particularly interested. On the other hand, in Southborough a good deal of information was provided and a good deal used. The role of the primary school staff generally seemed restricted to the technical details of choice, and guidance on selection and voluntary-aided matters.

The main aspects parents referred to as important when choosing schools were basically very similar across the four LEAs although the individual emphases varied greatly. The most important characteristic throughout was 'good standards of education/exam results/academic record'. It is possible though, that this is more of a limiting, or 'gating', factor than something parents look for to discriminate between schools. In other words as long as a school's standards are satisfactory then the parents may actually make the choice on other factors.

The issue of choice under different policies has a necessary codicil. It has been suggested in Chapter 4 that choice decisions may well be taken earlier than at the time the authority sends out its forms and so forth. The project asked the parents if they knew what school they had wanted *before* the child's last year in primary school. On average 71 per cent of the parents had known, a figure which varies little across the LEAs except for Southborough where it drops to 62 per cent. Furthermore, approximately 86 per cent of all these parents' children finally attended the school that they had thought of a year or more earlier. What is perhaps a little startling, is that of those who knew what school they wanted more than a year before, only approximately 4 per cent changed their minds during the last year in primary school. As overall 21 per cent of parents said they did not know what school they wanted a year before, and 4 per cent said that they had changed their mind, we can see that the active outcomes of all these procedures related only to about 25 per cent of parents. However it might well be just as important for the others to have had their opinions confirmed as for the 25 per cent to have participated. A positive decision to attend the school already thought of may be as important in educational terms as positively selecting an alternative school.

CHAPTER 6

Parents' Responses to Individual Schools

The previous chapter showed how the parents' responses to choosing a school varied according to their family circumstances, the LEA context and the local admissions procedures. However, parents' responses were also found to differ according to a fourth factor – the school their child eventually attended. This chapter concentrates on this last feature and looks at each of the four LEAs in turn, exploring how different types of school and school practices appeared to influence parents' responses.

Shiretown LEA

Shiretown LEA was a fully comprehensive, largely rural authority with few towns and a series of widely dispersed village schools. For a great many parents in the LEA therefore, the transfer of their child to anything but the nearest village school would have been totally impracticable. However, whilst this authority had been chosen because the research aimed to investigate the parents' perceptions of choice in rural areas, there was obviously little point in selecting an area which was so isolated that there was only one school for miles around. The project team thus selected an area which included a small ex-county town with two mixed comprehensive schools, and two outlying villages each with its own mixed comprehensive school (see map: Figure 6.1). Two other schools, to the south of the town, were near enough to feature in the considerations of some parents, but these schools were not included in the study.

Each of the four case-study schools had its own well-defined and discrete catchment area and the LEA provided transport only to the catchment-area school for those pupils who lived more than three miles away. Before transfer, all parents were informed that a place had been reserved for their child at the catchment-area school, and that no further action was needed unless they wished to express a preference for an alternative school. Approximately 80 per cent of the two town schools' pupils attended their catchment-area school compared with about 93 per cent for the two village schools.[1] Of the 70 per cent of parents who knew which school they wanted more than a year before transfer, approximately 90 per cent reported that their child now attended that school, and the LEA reported that there were no parents that year who did not eventually get a school which they had requested.

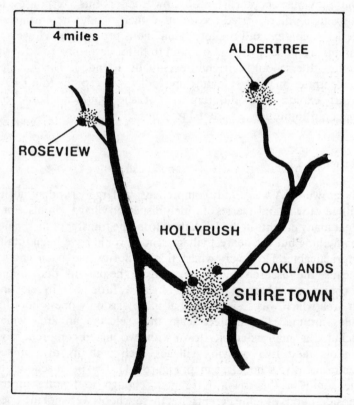

Figure 6.1:   Location of Shiretown schools

---

[1] Unless otherwise indicated all figures in the chapter relate to the academic year 1983/4.

Although each of the two town schools had a good reputation, one was said to have a much better one than the other. This school, Hollybush, was an 11 to 18 nine-form entry school[2] which was formerly the county grammar school and dated back several centuries. It was an impressive building, situated in an area of parkland just outside the town centre. Oaklands School was also a nine-form entry, 11 to 18 school, but was an ex-secondary modern school which was in the town itself, close by a large council estate. The head of Oaklands, who had been appointed at the time of comprehensive reorganization in 1970, had set about the task of establishing a new image for the school, based upon strict discipline and school uniform in order to compete with the lingering grammar school ethos of Hollybush.

When catchment areas were being drawn up for the newly reorganized comprehensive schools, the LEA had set about a degree of social engineering in an attempt to establish a comparable social mix in the intake of the two town schools. Thus they drew up the catchment-area boundaries so that a proportion of council estate pupils were in Hollybush's catchment area, even though they lived nearer to Oaklands School, and vice versa. In practice however, the LEA found that many of the council estate parents opted back to Oaklands School; a move which then enabled parents in the more affluent residential areas to opt for Hollybush School.

The two town schools, because of their different backgrounds and characteristics, clearly provided scope for the project team to explore the possible variations between the views of their respective parents. The two village schools were of interest because they too were apparently dissimilar, and also because one of them, Roseview, had some connection with the town situation. This arose because Roseview was a four-form entry school without a sixth form. Thus those wishing to go on to a sixth-form course could choose between either of the two town comprehensive schools or could elect to go to a technical college in another town ten miles away in the opposite direction. Apparently without exception, pupils who went to Shiretown for their sixth-form education chose the popular Hollybush School. Apart from the effect on the size of Hollybush's sixth form, this long-standing tradition had another

---

[2] A form of entry usually means 30 pupils. Hence Hollybush's intake is likely to be approximately 270 pupils in the first year.

important implication: school buses for sixth formers were laid on between Roseview village and Hollybush and parents of younger children who opted for and obtained a place at Hollybush could make use of this transport at a reduced rate. The head of Roseview believed that this facility, combined with the school's lack of a sixth form, encouraged a number of parents to opt for Hollybush School when their child was transferring at 11 years.

Roseview School itself had certain other important features. Having been built 20 years earlier as a small secondary modern school, it had become a viable comprehensive school only through a generous staffing and capitation allowance from the local authority. It had also been developed as a community school, serving the locality with sports, leisure and adult education activities on a large scale. The head, who had been in the post since the school opened, was extremely committed to the concept of community schools and appeared to have developed this aspect well.

Aldertree was the second village school, and was an 11 to 14, nine-form entry, ex-secondary modern school. It was perhaps the most rurally isolated of any of the schools included in the research, and transport was naturally limited. All its pupils transferred to the neighbouring 14 to 18 school which was run completely separately. Although designated as a community school, it had limited resources, and its position on the outskirts of the village further detracted from the possibility of it occupying a central role in community life.

In exploring the social background of the parents of the four schools, it was found that the fathers of Hollybush's first-year pupils had, on average, continued their full-time education approximately one year longer than fathers from the other three schools, and also that they had a marginally higher job status on the National Readership Survey Classification (Monk, 1978).

Choice of Schools

Of major interest to the project team were parents' views as to the amount of choice of school they felt they had had, and whether this differed between town and village schools, or between village schools and so on. Table 6.1 shows the variations in parental opinions.

Table 6.1: 'Do you feel you were offered a choice of schools for your child?'

	YES	NO	BLANK	TOTAL	
	%	%	%	%	N
Hollybush	30	65	6	101*	246
Oaklands	33	62	5	100	270
Roseview	33	52	15	100	129
Aldertree	14	78	8	100	247

*Where percentages add up to just over or just under 100%, this is due to the rounding-off of percentages.

Whilst the majority of all parents clearly felt that they did not have a choice, many more of Aldertree's parents felt this to be the case than in the other schools. This is as one might expect, since it was the most inaccessible of the four schools. However it is interesting to discover that among those parents who felt that they had most choice were Roseview's, since they were also in a fairly isolated village locality. It might be that the facility of using sixth-formers' buses to Hollybush enhanced their perceptions of choice.

When those parents who said that they had not had a choice were asked why they said this, differences in emphasis between the four schools became apparent. (Appendix: Table 6.1.) Most significantly only 13 per cent of Roseview's parents said that only one school had been offered, compared with between 21 and 29 per cent of parents from the other three schools. The table also suggests that bus services and/or travel arrangements proved more of an obstacle for the two village schools' parents than the two town schools' parents. Both Hollybush and Oaklands' parents gave comparable responses about why they felt they had had no choice except on one point: many more Oaklands' parents said that they were told by primary school staff or head that they had to attend the school. The project team was unfortunately unable to discover any real explanation for this curiously high percentage – no single primary school stood out as having more parents mentioning this than any other contributory primary school.

Parents from the two town schools also differed from the two village schools when asked about expressing a preference for an alternative school. It seems reasonable to assume that the higher percentage of parents from the two town schools, Hollybush and Oaklands, who did not accept their reserved place were more able

to consider choosing another school because the distances involved
and problems with buses would not be as great as for the village
parents (see Table 6.2). This would appear to be reinforced by the
higher proportion of village parents who did not respond to this
question at all – possibly because they failed to see the point of it.

Table 6.2: 'Did you accept the school that the authority first offered you?'

	YES	NO	BLANK
	%	%	%
Hollybush	80	15	5
Oaklands	73	21	6
Roseview	86	3	12
Aldertree	84	3	13

Reasons for Choosing Schools

A main concern of this research was to discover parents' reasons for
preferring particular schools more than others. Thus the
questionnaire asked 'What aspects were most important to you
when choosing a school?' It was felt that this format would enable
parents to raise points which might not relate to the school their
child was attending and would therefore provide information of
interest to many schools, rather than just those schools involved in
the research. However in Shiretown, where all the parents
eventually received the school they asked for, and only 24 parents
did not ask for the school they wanted, it seems likely that the
responses parents gave related fairly closely to the specific school
their child was attending. Thus, given that Hollybush was said to be
the most prestigious school with a good reputation, Hollybush
parents responded as one might have expected; i.e. the majority of
them mentioned academic record (56 per cent), followed a long way
behind by discipline (38 per cent), before the vague, but
nevertheless important, references to its being 'a good school' (23
per cent).(See Table 6.3. A more complete list is available upon
request – see Appendix 3.1.)

Oaklands' parents' responses also reflected the popular image of
the school (see page 115) in that more of them referred to discipline
(56 per cent) than academic record (49 per cent). The fact that the

Table 6.3: The five aspects which were most important to Shiretown parents when choosing a school (A complete list is available – see Appendix 3.1)

%	Hollybush	Oaklands	Roseview	Aldertree
55	academic record	discipline		
50		academic record		academic record
45			academic record	discipline
40	discipline			
35				
30				
25	good school	staff/head		
20	many subject options staff/head		discipline school size staff/head	
15				access/travel good school facilities staff/head

school was close by was also obviously important to Oaklands' parents (37 per cent) and supported the LEA's opinion that the council estate parents viewed Oaklands as 'their' school by virtue of its proximity.

Turning to the village schools, although the majority of Roseview's parents who responded to this question mentioned the importance of academic record (46 per cent), a fairly high proportion also considered its proximity important (37 per cent). The fact that Roseview was an extremely small school (four forms of entry compared to nine in the other three schools), is also reflected in its parents' responses – 20 per cent said school size was an important consideration in choosing a school.

Aldertree's parents' responses are somewhat harder to explain. Whilst academic record (52 per cent) and discipline (43 per cent) featured highly in the aspects considered important when choosing a school, it was a little surprising, particularly given earlier responses indicating difficulties of transport, that only 17 per cent mentioned access or travel as being important.

Influences on Choice and Uses of School Information

Obviously at the time when parents had to make decisions about their child's future school, many will have been interested in all the information at their disposal. This would include not only official information, such as LEA and school brochures, examination results, parents' evenings, and so forth, but also the views of others, such as friends and teachers, and of course the views of their own children. These aspects are considered individually over the next few pages.

THE CHILD

When Shiretown parents were asked whether their child had felt strongly about which school he or she went to, the majority of parents in all but Aldertree School indicated that their child had had strong views (see Table 6.4). It seems likely that Aldertree children, like their parents, perceived that they had little choice and therefore did not express an opinion.

Table 6.4:   'Did your child feel strongly about which school he or she went to?'

	YES %	NO %	BLANK %
Hollybush	52	44	4
Oaklands	65	33	2
Roseview	52	44	4
Aldertree	39	56	5

WHO PARENTS TALKED TO ABOUT THE CHOICE OF SCHOOL

Parents were asked to state with whom they had discussed the choice of school (see Appendix: Table 6.2). Once again Aldertree parents' responses differed from those of the other three schools' parents in that fewer of them claimed to have talked with other people, indeed, as many as 50 per cent of Aldertree parents did not discuss the choice of school with anyone at all. It seems most likely that this is again linked to the feeling of not having had a choice of school. Quite naturally parents who felt they had no say in the matter would be less likely to seek discussions on secondary schools. Another interesting feature is that a higher percentage of Roseview parents compared with parents in other schools, appear to have discussed the choice of school with other parents. A possible explanation for this may be the amount of community activity in Roseview School which gave parents more chance to meet and discuss such issues.

SCHOOL VISITS/TALKS

It appears that only Oaklands School organized a parents' evening prior to the closing date for expressing a preference. However, this event was tailored to suit where parents lived: one parents' evening was held in the school for town parents, and two were in contributory primary schools for village parents. Whilst only catchment-area parents were invited to these occasions, the fact that they were organized at all demonstrates Oaklands' awareness of the need to maintain a high public profile at the time of transfer, especially in the light of Hollybush's well-known popularity.

The heads of the other three secondary schools told the project team that they were happy to show parents around the school, but that this was only done upon demand; the heads would not initiate these occasions themselves. Given this situation, one might have expected that more of Oaklands' parents would have attended at least one parents' evening prior to choice than parents from the other three schools. However, this does not appear to have been the case as Table 6.5 shows, though these figures may not give a fair representation as two of the Oaklands' parents' evenings were held in primary schools and not at the secondary school and these were 'talks' rather than 'visits'. The 'fact that more Roseview parents visited at least one school before choice might be explained by its being an active community school and therefore more parents were likely to visit it for purposes not directly connected with school transfer.

Table 6.5: 'How many schools did you visit before choice?'

	Hollybush	Oaklands	Roseview	Aldertree
	%	%	%	%
none	60	56	45	62
one	24	28	43	30
two	6	6	5	0
three or more	3	2	1	2
visited at least one	33	36	49	32

Parents who visited at least one school prior to choice were asked how useful they found the visit. A higher percentage of Oaklands School parents found them useful than parents at the other three schools (see Appendix: Table 6.3). This is possibly explained by the fact that the visit was an organized occasion at which parents were shown round the whole school by pupils and were then given a formal talk by the head.

SCHOOL BROCHURES

There was some variation between the four schools in the publication and distribution of their school brochures. It appears that both Aldertree and Hollybush Schools sent only one copy to each of their contributory primary schools, and parents who wanted their own copy had to request it. Oaklands School on the other hand said that each catchment-area parent received a brochure via the primary school, prior to the final date for expressing a preference. Roseview Community School did not distribute their 'DES regulations booklet' but made this available on request. However, being a community school, it produced several publications for the whole community, one of which, *The School Prospectus*, was annually hand-delivered to every household in the village.

These variations in the availability of published information seem to be reflected in the parents' responses such that 62 per cent of

Roseview parents had seen at least one brochure compared with 56 per cent of Oaklands parents, and between 30 and 40 per cent of the other two groups of parents. (See Appendix: Table 6.4.) The parents' responses to this question also show that once again fewer Aldertree parents sought information on alternative schools – again this is probably linked with the perception of having no choice.

PUBLISHED EXAMINATION RESULTS

Parents were asked how many different schools' public examination results they had seen before choice. Since Aldertree School was an 11 to 14 school, and relevant results were published only in the neighbouring 14 to 18 school's brochure, naturally fewer Aldertree parents saw any external exam results. For the other three schools, although approximately similar percentages of parents saw at least one set of results (i.e. between 30 and 40 per cent), it is noticeable that many more parents from Hollybush School, the school with supposedly the highest academic reputation, saw three or more sets of examination results. This might be taken to be confirmation of their greater concern with academic reputation as indicated in Table 6.3, or else, more simply, that their local paper was more active in publishing exam results. Of those Hollybush parents who saw exam results, 95 per cent saw them in the press compared with 65 per cent at Oaklands, 40 per cent at Roseview and 33 per cent at Aldertree. (See Appendix: Table 6.5.)

Summary

In Shiretown LEA there were numerous examples of parents from the four schools reacting differently to many of the processes involved in allocation to secondary school. Although the majority of parents from each school felt that they had not had a choice of school, Aldertree parents felt this most strongly. This seems to be reflected in the fact that fewer of their children had strong views about the choice of school, and that virtually all of them attended the school which the authority first offered. Also, far fewer of Aldertree's parents consulted anyone about the choice of school, visited any school before the closing date for expressing a preference, or saw a school brochure or set of examination results before that time.

In view of Aldertree's geographic isolation it is understandable that many parents felt they had had little choice. Curiously however, parents from the other village school, Roseview, felt there to be no less choice than in the two town schools. Perhaps as was suggested by the head of Roseview the possibility of travelling on the sixth-formers' buses to Hollybush School had something to do with this feeling. The parents' greater perception of choice was echoed by their greater use of the information provided although this may be because of the community's involvement in the school which promoted accessibility to the school, to other parents and to various forms of published information. The fact that more parents from Roseview mentioned a concern with where the child would be happy may also be linked with the community school aspect, since their children may also have been more familiar with the school, and therefore parents may have envisaged them settling in more easily.

Oaklands School's parents were noticeably the most concerned with good discipline – something for which the school was known to have a reputation. Also, a high proportion of its parents felt distance between home and school to be important. It was apparent however that many of its parents had not simply accepted their catchment-area school – more parents from Oaklands than from any other school indicated that they had refused the school which the authority had first offered them. This demonstrates the trend that the LEA had initially described whereby those council estate parents who had been placed in Hollybush's catchment area opted back to their local school.

Parents from Hollybush School were most noticeable for their emphasis on the importance of a school's reputation. Given that Hollybush was an ex-grammar school with good facilities, a large, well-established sixth form, extremely attractive buildings and surroundings, it might have been expected that more parents would have raised these points. However it seems that, for all this, relatively few of its parents visited any schools, saw any brochures, or consulted other people about the choice of school. Only with regard to published examination results did Hollybush parents emerge as more informed in that almost twice as many of them saw three or more sets of examination results or more.

Seatown LEA

Seatown was a profitable county town with its own light industry as well as being sufficiently accessible to London to fall within its commuter belt. The town had seven mixed 11 to 18 comprehensive schools (including one Roman Catholic school) and two single-sex, county grammar schools. In order to take into account as many considerations as possible, i.e. selection, denomination and popularity, the project chose five of these schools for its case studies: the girls' grammar school, the Roman Catholic comprehensive school and three of the state maintained comprehensive schools, two which were very popular and one which was unpopular but which had begun to improve its image.

The LEA, in support of its policy of community-based education, strongly favoured catchment areas for its comprehensive schools. All parents living in the Seatown area were told that a place had been reserved for their child at their catchment-area school, and that they need 'take no further action unless they wished to request an alternative school, to enter their child for the 11+ examination, or to do both. The two single-sex grammar schools operated on a county basis and did not have clearly defined catchment areas. The voluntary-aided Roman Catholic school equally had a very large catchment area which was based on the diocesan organization and covered the whole of Seatown and surrounding countryside.

Between 85 and 90 per cent of Seatown pupils attended their catchment-area school in 1983/4, and approximately half the pupil population was entered for the 11+ examination. The LEA paid for, or provided, transport to the catchment-area school, grammar, or Roman Catholic school if the pupils lived more than three miles away. Parents of non-Roman Catholic children who attended the Roman Catholic school had to pay the first £20 towards travel costs.

The Five Schools

The Girls' County High School was a three-form entry grammar school which took approximately 2 per cent from the top 10 per cent of the ability range. (The equivalent boys' grammar school took the same percentage of the boys' ability range.) Parents had to decide by November of their child's last year of primary school whether they intended to enter their child for the 11+ examination.

In considering the social background of the parents of the five schools, the project team found that both mothers and fathers of first-year grammar school pupils had, on average, continued their full-time education approximately two years longer than parents from the other four schools, and that the fathers of the grammar school pupils had on average a higher job status on the National Readership scale than fathers of pupils in the other schools.

St Paul's Roman Catholic Comprehensive School was a popular, six-form entry school. Prior to 1975, when it had been a secondary modern school which shared a site with the technical high school, it was reported to have had a rather poor reputation. Since then, the changeover to comprehensive education and the appointment of a new head seemed to have increased its popularity considerably. There were a number of non-Roman Catholic parents who also applied to the school each year, a small percentage of whom were usually taken.

The three state maintained comprehensive schools were chosen to highlight a range of popularity and situations. Newcrest Comprehensive School was an extremely popular, eight-form entry school with modern buildings. It was reported to have a traditional and academic image even though a considerable proportion of its catchment-area pupils (between 7 and 8 per cent) were 'creamed-off' by the grammar schools. This was argued by the LEA to arise because of its proximity to both grammar schools and because of its mainly middle-class catchment area. Another interesting feature of the school was that although it was co-educational, boys and girls were taught in separate classes for the first three years. LEA officers said that many parents outside the catchment-area mentioned 'single-sex' education as a reason for preferring this school. However, some officers suspected that since 'preference for single-sex or co-educational schools' was one of the LEA's published criteria for school admissions, this was merely a ploy to gain admission to the school rather than a real desire for single-sex education.

Steepleton Comprehensive School was a six-form entry school which was formed in 1975 by the merger of a secondary modern school and a technical high school. It was described by LEA officers as having a good reputation locally, though marginally less popularity than Newcrest School. It was said to emphasize Christian values as well as promoting the image of specializing in music.

The fifth school, Hawthorn Comprehensive, was selected because it was an unpopular school which was just beginning to change its image. It was felt that the contrast between Hawthorn and its neighbour, Steepleton, would be an interesting situation to study. Hawthorn was a five-form entry school, situated in a council estate and up to two years earlier it had had a very poor reputation which the previous headteacher had done little to combat. Since that time, a new head had been appointed and both education officers and parents had described him as being very dynamic and commented that he had made a considerable, and most favourable, impact on the school's image and activities. However, at the time of the research, the old reputation still lingered somewhat in neighbouring catchment areas.

Choice of Schools

As was mentioned in the previous section, the project team was most interested in the parents' perceptions of the choice available to them. Given the range of types of schools in Seatown and the LEA's emphasis on catchment areas it is perhaps not surprising that there was a difference in the amount of choice parents felt they had been offered (see Table 6.6).

Table 6.6:   'Do you feel you were offered a choice of schools for your child?'

	YES	NO	BLANK	TOTAL	
	%	%	%	%	N
Girls' County High	63	33	4	100	84
St Paul's R.C.	54	41	6	101	137
Newcrest	52	37	12	101	224
Hawthorn	41	54	5	100	120
Steepleton	38	52	10	100	150

Although between a third and a half of parents reported that they had felt they had no choice, few of them gave reasons for this response. One might assume that the higher percentage of parents from the Girls' High School who felt that they had had a choice was due to their child's having passed the 11+ examination and hence presenting a choice of either grammar or comprehensive education.

In the same way, Roman Catholic parents could be seen to have an extra choice becasue they were offered their catchment-area school, but they could also choose the Roman Catholic school and still enter their child for the 11+ as well. The parents' response is supported by the fact that when asked whether they had accepted the school first offered by the authority, fewer parents with children at the Roman Catholic school or the Girls' High School claimed to have done so – i.e. more of them had actually exercised a choice. However, not all Roman Catholic or Girls' High School parents felt that they had had a choice. Roughly half of those parents in these two schools indicated that they had not been given an option and some said that this was because they had only been offered one school. One grammar school parent commented that:

> There is no real choice. Two per cent of children can gain places at grammar schools in this area, if they are fortunate enough to pass the 11+ exam. Failing this, there is no alternative to the local catchment area comprehensive school.

Reasons for Choosing Schools

As in the previous LEA, the aspects which were important to parents when choosing a school in Seatown could be seen to vary according to which school their child was attending. However, there appears to be a general, though not totally consistent pattern: the more choice parents perceived they had, the more highly they rated academic record and the more widely spread were the aspects they listed. Thus the Girls' High School parents' first five responses ranged from 68 to 13 per cent whilst Steepleton's parents ranged between only 46 and 22 per cent. Beyond this seeming pattern, individual schools revealed certain other interesting points. (See Table 6.7. A more complete list is available upon request – see Appendix 3.1.)

Table 6.7: The first five aspects which were most important to Seatown parents when choosing a school (A complete list is available – see Appendix 3.1)

%	Girls' High	St Paul's RC	Newcrest	Hawthorn	Steepleton
70	academic record				
65			academic record		
60		academic record discipline			
55					
50					
45		denomin- ational		proximity	academic record
40	discipline	staff/head		academic record	
35				staff/head	facilities discipline
30					
25			facilities proximity	discipline	good school
20	Child's academic needs facilities	proximity	access/ travel	good school	access/ travel
15	academic atmosphere single-sex wide subject choice clubs/ activities				

Not surprisingly, the vast majority of parents of children attending the Girls' High School found the school's academic record an important consideration (68 per cent). There was then a huge drop to the next most important aspect – that of discipline (39 per cent). Following this, a similarly large gap then occurred before a cluster of other aspects emerged of which many also emphasized academic concerns; namely, the matching of the school with the child's academic needs, the academic atmosphere, the wide choice of subject options, the qualities of the staff and possibly the fact that the school was single sex.

One might have imagined that amongst St Paul's School's parents the denominational aspect would be a major consideration. However, less than half of its parents mentioned this aspect. Instead academic record again took priority, followed again, but this time more closely, by discipline. It seems likely that the school's popularity with non-Roman Catholic parents was linked to this emphasis on academic standards, and certainly, more Roman Catholic parents placed the school's academic reputation before its denominational aspect.

Out of the three state comprehensive schools, Newcrest was the one which was earlier described as having a traditional and academic reputation. This would seem to be reflected in the parents' major concern for academic record and discipline. This impression is also confirmed by the relatively low emphasis on proximity and travel, although more parents mentioned this feature than did Roman Catholic or Girls' High School parents.

On the other hand, proximity to the school was the most commonly mentioned factor by Hawthorn School's parents. As Hawthorn was situated in an area of council housing this was perhaps to be expected since costs of travel were likely to be of greater concern for low income families. Also, academic reputation was mentioned by a lower percentage of Hawthorn's parents than parents from any of the other four schools. This again would seem to reflect the local situation in that Hawthorn School had previously been an unpopular school with a poor reputation, although it was currently struggling to improve its academic image. Interestingly Hawthorn's third most commonly mentioned factor involved positive descriptors of the head or staff – a point which was raised earlier as having been commented on by the LEA officers and a number of parents who were interviewed.

Influences on Parents' Choices and Their Use of School Information

THE CHILD

In Shiretown LEA the parents' perception of lack of choice followed the same pattern as their child's views, i.e. the fewer the parents who felt they had a choice, the fewer children who had strong views about which school. In Seatown this was not always the case. Parents at both Steepleton and Hawthorn had similar feelings about the amount of choice, but at Hawthorn School the number of children who had felt strongly about going to the school was far lower than at Steepleton or any of the other schools (see Table 6.8). It is difficult to see why this difference should be so pronounced, unless it is based upon different reasons for there being little choice. It could be argued that Hawthorn was poorly thought of and that Steepleton was inaccessible to Hawthorn parents. Therefore Hawthorn parents perceived little choice. Steepleton parents may have perceived little choice because they did not regard Hawthorn as a viable choice. For the children going to Steepleton it would be an attractive proposition whereas Hawthorn would not engender the same feelings.

Table 6.8: **'Did your child feel strongly about which school he or she went to?'**

	YES	NO	BLANK
	%	%	%
Girls' High	71	27	2
St Paul's	75	24	1
Newcrest	70	26	4
Hawthorn	56	43	1
Steepleton	72	25	3

WHO PARENTS TALKED TO ABOUT THE CHOICE OF SCHOOL

It appears that once again there is a link between how many people the parents discussed the choice of school with and the amount of perceived choice (see Appendix: Table 6.2). For example, only 10 per cent of the Girls' High School parents claimed to have not talked to anyone, compared with 14 per cent of the Roman Catholic School parents, and 29 per cent of Steepleton parents. Although the pattern is not absolutely consistent, it is nevertheless visible. It seems therefore, and not unreasonably so, that the more choice parents felt they had, the more they found it worthwhile discussing the situation. Conversely, the less choice parents felt they had, the less inclined they appear to have been to discuss the matter.

SCHOOL VISITS/TALKS

All but the Girls' High School gave a talk or held an open evening prior to parents having to express a preference. Steepleton School gave a talk at the school whereas staff from Newcrest and St Paul's visited parents in their children's primary school. Furthermore, the head or deputy of St Paul's actually interviewed all of their prospective parents. Hawthorn School, which was most concerned to improve its reputation, held an 'open week' in which talks were presented and sixth-formers gave guided tours. For the three state comprehensive schools, invitations to all these occasions were limited to catchment-area parents only.

The pattern of parents attending school talks and/or visiting secondary schools is shown in Table 6.9. It is not particularly surprising that whilst at least half of the parents from each of the four comprehensive schools visited their child's school before the closing date for expressing a preference, only a quarter of the Girls' High School's parents did the same. Indeed this could be considered a fairly high proportion given the fact that they had to initiate a visit themselves and presumably make it during the daytime. The fact that higher percentages of parents from the comprehensive than grammar schols had elder children in the same school meant that more of the comprehensive school parents were likely to have already visited these schools in connection with their elder child, but this could not account for the size of the discrepancy in numbers visiting schools.

When looking at the number of parents who visited more than one school, or more than one talk, Table 6.9 would seem to confirm the point which has been repeatedly made – that more of the grammar school and Roman Catholic school parents felt that they had had a choice. This is indicated in the fact that 19 per cent of them visited two schools before choice, compared with an average of only 6 per cent in the other three schools, and a further 11 per

Table 6.9: **Seatown parents' attendance at school visits or school talks**

	Girls' High	St Paul's	Newcrest	Hawthorn	Steepleton
	%	%	%	%	%
'How many schools did you visit before you had to choose?'					
none	39	38	49	43	40
one	29	34	41	49	48
two	19	19	5	5	9
three or more	11	5	2	1	1
'Did you visit the school your child now goes to before you had to choose?'*					
Yes	25	74	62	54	68
No	73	23	34	44	29
'Did you go to any other talks about secondary schools?' (Other than the one your child now attends)					
Yes	52	22	15	5	15
No	45	15	82	94	82

*Possibly the discrepancy between the responses to this question and the previous one is due to parents forgetting that the question specified 'before you had to choose'.

cent of grammar school parents visited three schools or more. A similar pattern can also be seen in the attendance at school talks. The clear implication is that where parents felt they had a choice, they made greater efforts to compare schools and exercise that choice.

SCHOOL BROCHURES

As with parents' evenings, all but the Girls' High School provided written information for parents prior to their having to express a preference. School brochures from each of the four comprehensive schools were distributed via primary schools, or were available at the school talks, but again these were offered to catchment-area parents only. The Girls' High School had a brochure which was available upon request.

Parents were asked how many brochures they had read before choosing, so that the responses, of course, may not necessarily relate to their own school's brochure. Once more the Girls' High and Roman Catholic schools' parents had seen more brochures than parents from the other three schools: these parents seeing an average of approximately 1.3 brochures each compared with about 0.7 each at the other three schools (see Appendix: Table 6.4).

PUBLISHED EXAMINATION RESULTS

Finally, when looking at the number of sets of examination results seen before choice, it is evident that the trend of the grammar and Roman Catholic school parents seeking more information on alternative schools continues. It is also evident that the parents from Newcrest School, where a traditional academic image was portrayed, were similarly keen to see several sets of examination results. That so few Steepleton parents saw any results is surprising although the facts that the press published little in this way and that the exam results were only available upon demand may be partly responsible (see Appendix: Table 6.5).

Summary

It seems when looking at the perceptions and activities of parents from the five schools in Seatown, that these were often related to the amount of choice parents perceived that they had. Thus it can be argued that both the Girls' High School and St Paul's R.C. School parents talked to more people about choosing schools, saw more brochures and examination results, and attended more talks on alternative schools because more of them felt that they had had a choice to make.

Perhaps surprisingly, given their ranging reputations and situations, the three 'ordinary' comprehensive schools did not appear to have attracted parents with particularly different views, or to have encouraged vastly different levels of activity. On the whole, differences between the parents from these three schools were small, and, where they were apparent, were often difficult to explain.

Perhaps the most notable differences between parents from each of the five schools emerged on their considerations when choosing a school. Although the Girls' High and St Paul's School parents were basically similar in their perceptions of choice and approaches to finding out about several different schools, their responses to this question differed somewhat. Whilst academic record and/or examination results was the most commonly mentioned consideration in both schools, and was given by over 60 per cent in each, the Roman Catholic school parents seem almost equally concerned with good discipline, unlike the Girls' High School parents. Possibly parents of girls are less concerned with discipline than parents of boys. Also surprising was the relatively low percentage of St Paul's School parents who mentioned denominational considerations (less than half). Given that these parents must have chosen the Roman Catholic school in preference to their catchment-area school, the obvious assumptions that (a) parents who wanted a Roman Catholic education for their children still wanted to make sure that the school had a sound academic reputation and/or (b) for some parents, the qualities of St. Paul's School and staff, combined with the special transport provision and the opportunity of opting away from their catchment-area school, all combined to make it a more attractive option which was accessible to them as Catholics.

Turning to the three 'ordinary' comprehensives, it was notable that in the one with the traditional academic reputation, Newcrest, parents responded very similarly to St Paul's School parents, and that approximately twice as many of them referred to discipline than did in the other two state comprehensives.

Finally, Hawthorn School, which reputedly had the least popular image and for which pressure to opt away exceeded pressure to opt in, emerged as the only school where academic record was not the most frequently cited consideration. However the influence of the new head had already been recognized in that many parents mentioned the importance of the head and staff when choosing a school.

Northtown LEA

Northtown LEA was a widely spread, largely rural authority with several large towns. The changeover to comprehensive education had occurred in some areas in the 1970s, but had never been completed throughout the LEA. The research centred upon Northtown itself which had a selective system, and which was described both by LEA officers and local heads as an economically and socially depressed town. The research included all the main secondary schools which took pupils from the area; i.e. one mixed grammar school, three 11 to 16, mixed, secondary modern schools, and a comprehensive school in a neighbouring LEA. This last school, Riverview, was included because its catchment area partly overlapped with that of the grammar school, and thus it had an important impact upon the local transfer system. The map shows the locations of the five schools: see Figure 6.2.

The town's grammar school, Northtown High, was a four-form entry, 11 to 18 school which until two years earlier had comprised two small, single-sex grammar schools on the same site. At the time of the research, it appeared that the school was popular and had a good reputation. The three secondary modern schools were reported to be considerably less popular. Two of them, Birchtree and Ashfield, were in the town itself and shared a common catchment area. Birchtree was a three-form entry school and acknowledged by the head and LEA officers to be in a state of disrepair. Ashfield was a five-form entry school with less 'worn' buildings. Despite this, the LEA reported that popularity between these two schools fluctuated from year to year and that parents almost always chose the nearest school to their home. Neither school was able to identify any parents who had opted contrary to this pattern, apart from those parents who had moved house since their elder child had started at one of the secondary schools and who still wanted all their children to attend the same school. Cattleford Secondary Modern School was situated in a village three miles south of Northtown and was a three-form entry rural school. All its pupils came from the village of Cattleford or surrounding rural area and it received no pupils from the catchment area of the two town secondary modern schools.

Riverview Comprehensive School was in a neighbouring LEA, in a small village about 15 miles away from Northtown. It was a mixed, four-form entry, 11 to 16 school. Although it had originally been a secondary modern school, it had been extended to become comprehensive in 1968, and at the time of the research was a very popular school with many facilities and attractive new buildings.

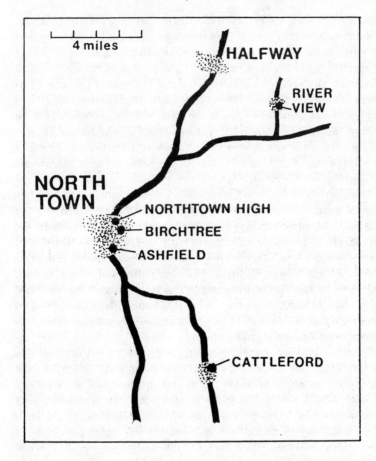

Figure 6.2: **Location of Northtown schools**

Those pupils wishing to do 'A' levels could choose either a sixth-form college or a sixth form in another comprehensive school in the same LEA.

The Riverview/Northtown Connection

Riverview Comprehensive School's catchment area was particularly unusual in that it included four villages which were in

Northtown LEA. Riverview had been built for the children of these villages which, prior to the 1974 boundary changes had all been part of the same, now non-existent authority. After the 1974 reorganization, it was agreed that the school should still automatically serve the children in three of the four villages. Thus these children did not take the 11+ examination and they continued, as a matter of course, to go to their local comprehensive school, albeit in another LEA. Only those in the fourth village, Halfway, were in an option zone, i.e. parents from this village could opt for either the selective system in Northtown or Riverview Comprehensive School.

Between 1974 and 1980, parents in Halfway who chose to enter their children for the 11+ examination were advised that they could not send them to the comprehensive school if they failed the exam, but that they would have to choose from one of the two Northtown secondary modern schools. Alternatively these parents could opt for Riverview Comprehensive School from the outset, i.e. before the 11+ was taken. The outcome of this system was that for several years the majority of parents from Halfway village chose not to enter their child for the 11+, and went as a matter of course to Riverview Comprehensive School.

With the passing of the 1980 Act, Riverview's LEA felt that this system could no longer be insisted upon, and anticipated that a three-tier system would emerge in which parents from Halfway Village would all aim for the grammar school in Northtown and then choose the comprehensive school if their child failed the 11+. In practice, this occurred to only a small extent and the majority of parents maintained their traditional allegiance to Riverview Comprehensive School. For example, in 1984, only 15 of the 48 Halfway Primary School final-year pupils took the 11+ examination.

However, since the Act came into being a small but steadily growing trickle of parents from Northtown itself have opted for Riverview School and have even organized their own, hired transport for the 15-mile journey. It was felt by the head of Riverview that these were most likely to be parents of borderline 11+ candidates who wanted to be sure of getting a place at the comprehensive school rather than sending their children to the secondary modern schools in their own town.

Choice of Schools

In the Northtown sample, the only parents who had an active choice to make, i.e. a choice which was not dependent solely upon the outcome of selection procedures, were (a) parents living in Northtown itself, who had to choose which of the two secondary modern schools they wanted in the event of their child failing the 11+, and (b) the parents of Halfway village who could choose to enter their child for the 11+ and/or opt for Riverview Comprehensive School. This situation is reflected in the parents' responses about whether they felt they had been offered a choice of school (see Table 6.10). The vast majority of parents from Ashfield and Birchtree Secondary Modern Schools felt that they had had a choice. Most Northtown High School parents also felt this and presumably for the same reason, i.e. that they had had to complete a 'choice' form. That less than half of Riverview parents felt they had had a choice is as one might expect, since only those living in Halfway village were given an active choice; the rest were not invited to express an opinion, but were informed that Riverview was their catchment-area school. Not surprisingly, very few of Cattleford's parents felt that they had had a choice; presumably they realized that the school their child attended was dependent upon the outcome of the 11+ and that neither 'passing' nor 'failing' gave rise to any further choice.

Table 6.10: 'Do you feel you were offered a choice of schools for your child?'

	YES	NO	BLANK	TOTAL	
	%	%	%	%	N
Northtown High School	70	25	5	100	118
Ashfield Secondary Modern	91	8	1	100	156
Birchtree Secondary Modern	81	17	2	100	78
Cattleford Secondary Modern	23	63	14	100	65
Riverview Comprehensive	44	42	14	100	125

Reasons for Choosing Schools

Parents were asked about what things they considered most important when choosing a school. Interestingly, the five most common responses from the selective school, Northtown High, show a similar pattern to those of the Seatown High School parents (which was also selective) – i.e. not only are the reasons featured in the same order, but more importantly, they are given similar emphasis (see Table 6.11). Thus 61 per cent of Northtown High School parents mentioned academic record (Seatown High = 39 per cent) followed by a cluster of other, mostly academically related aspects, listed by between 10 and 13 per cent (Seatown High = between 13 and 17 per cent).

Riverview Comprehensive School's parents mentioned academic record more than anything else, although the percentage was lower than that of the high school's. Again this was followed by discipline. However, a noticeably higher proportion of Riverview parents mentioned facilities and the qualities of the head and/or staff. This finding reinforced the feelings of a number of Northtown LEA officers about some of the reasons for the school's popularity. The parents from the two town secondary modern schools were most noticeable for their equal emphasis on proximity to the school – again reinforcing the LEA's belief that parents of children who have failed the 11+ choose a secondary modern primarily on the basis of where they lived.

Cattleford parents were perhaps most noticeable for the relatively low numbers of reasons they volunteered, i.e. they gave, on average, 1.5 reasons each compared with 2.8 per parent at the high school. Although academic record was the most commonly offered reason, it was mentioned by only 39 per cent of parents. Other reasons were mentioned by many fewer parents, 17 per cent and less. Once again it seems that the perceived lack of choice led to fewer parents even considering a choice of school, and hence responding to the question.

Influences on Parents' Choices and Their Use of School Information

THE CHILD

Table 6.12 shows the percentage of parents whose child felt strongly about the choice of school. Again we see the same trend emerging as that of Shiretown's responses – namely that the less the parents perceived there to be a choice the less strongly their child felt about the school they attended. It seems that the amount of choice offered was an influence on children's feelings just as it affected the parents.

Table 6.11: The first five aspects which were most important to Northtown parents when choosing a school (A complete list is available – see Appendix 3.1)

%	Northtown	Birchtree	Ashfield	Cattleford	Riverview
60	academic record				
55					academic record
50					
45		proximity	proximity		
40	discipline			academic record	discipline
35					
30			academic record		
25		academic record	discipline		head/staff facilities
20		access/travel sibling connections good school staff/head	good school	discipline staff/head access/travel facilities where child will be happy	
15	good school facilities wide subject choice child's academic needs staff/head		facilities		good reputation proximity

Table 6.12:   'Did your child feel strongly about which school he or she went to?'

	YES %	NO %	BLANK %
Northtown High School	75	23	2
Birchtree Secondary Modern	69	31	0
Ashfield Secondary Modern	76	21	3
Cattleford Secondary Modern	32	59	9
Riverview Comprehensive	62	34	4

WHO PARENTS TALKED TO ABOUT THE CHOICE OF SCHOOL

Once again there is an apparent link between those parents who felt they had least choice, in this case, Cattleford, and those who did not discuss the matter at all (see Appendix: Table 6.2). However the opposite did not necessarily hold; parents from the two town secondary modern schools were the ones who most felt they had had a choice, yet they are second only to Cattleford in not discussing the schools with anyone. A different factor appears to have been at play here – namely that the secondary modern schools' parents did not feel the need to discuss their choice, because the main concern for most of them was proximity, a criterion which they could easily assess for themselves.

Looking beyond the percentages of parents who did not talk to anyone, the high school's parents talked to more people overall about the choice of school than did the parents from the other schools. Apart from consulting their 11-year-old child, they most commonly mentioned the staff and head of their child's primary/ junior school – possibly this is because they were more concerned to know whether their child was suited to a grammar school education, or what their child's chances were of passing the 11+.

SCHOOL VISITS/TALKS

It appears that only Riverview Comprehensive School held a parents' evening prior to choice, and even here, parents from the 'option village', i.e. Halfway Village, were invited. The head explained that the purpose of the evening was to help these parents to make up their minds about entering their child for the 11+ and this was why it was held some 18 months before transfer. Table 6.13 shows the percentage of parents who visited any schools before choice.

Table 6.13: 'How many schools did you visit before choice?'

	Northtown High	Birchtree Sec. Mod.	Ashfield Sec. Mod.	Cattleford Sec. Mod.	Riverview Comp.
Schools visited:	%	%	%	%	%
none	80	89	83	69	57
one	10	8	11	20	31
two	6	3	1	5	6
three or more	1	0	0	0	2

Since the majority of option zone parents opted for Riverview School each year and this school invited these parents to a parents' evening, it is not particularly surprising that many more Riverview parents visited prospective schools than did parents from other schools where less than 25 per cent of the parents actually visited their child's prospective school before choice. Given the grammar school's parents' concern to consult with primary school staff, one might have anticipated that more of them would have visited at least one school. It may be that many parents took it for granted that a grammar school was a good school by definition.

SCHOOL BROCHURES

Again it appears that only Riverview Comprehensive School distributed any written information about the school prior to choice. This information comprised the school's termly newspaper which was circulated to each child in the catchment area during their last year in primary school. Furthermore, parents in Halfway Village (i.e. in the option zone) received Riverview's school brochure at the end of their child's penultimate year in primary school. The two Northtown town secondary modern schools provided their main contributory primary schools with a stock of brochures should any parents request them, whilst Cattleford Secondary Modern School's brochure (which only consisted of stapled A4 sheets) was only available from Cattleford School on request. The High School also only provided its brochure upon request.

Once again these variations in procedure are reflected in the numbers of brochures the parents reported seeing. Thus, more Riverview parents saw at least one brochure (49 per cent compared with between 30 and 40 per cent at the other schools – see Appendix: Table 6.4), and with exam results 35 per cent of Riverview and High School parents saw at least one set compared with less than 20 per cent in each of the other three schools (Appendix: Table 6.5). This reinforces the latter parents' seeming academic orientation which emerged in many of their responses. However as with Shiretown the influence of the local press cannot be ignored. The majority of Riverview parents' saw exam results in the school's brochure whereas the grammar school's results were mostly seen in the press.

Summary

There was considerable variation in the amount of choice that parents from each of the five schools felt there to be. This appears to reflect the varying allocation procedures encountered by the different groups of parents. One thing seems certain; despite the theoretical debate as to whether a choice between like schools constitutes a real choice, many parents in Northtown felt they had been offered a choice. The overwhelming majority of parents from the town's two secondary modern schools had actually had to state a choice between two schools and had felt that there had been a choice. Very few of the Cattleford Secondary Modern School parents felt the same way.

In Northtown LEA, as with Shiretown and Seatown, it was evident that where parents felt that they had not had a choice, they they did not pursue discussions with school staff, and their children were reported as not holding strong views about which school they wanted to go to. Furthermore, as in the other two LEAs, low perceptions of choice were reinforced by low attendance at school visits and the low take-up of written information. However, the converse was not always true. The feeling of choice in Northtown did not necessarily result in much information being used, but then one would need to consider the type of choice on offer and the availability of the information – issues that appear very strikingly in the fourth LEA, Southborough.

Southborough LEA

Within the London borough of Southborough there were 23 maintained secondary schools. A number of these were voluntary aided and two in this group were organized as selective girls' schools. Thus whilst the vast majority of schools were comprehensive, there was some selection for girls and there were several public schools in the immediate vicinity. The borough could not, therefore, be described as fully comprehensive. With respect to 'choice', for many years Southborough had been operating on an 'optimal choice' system and as such there were no catchment areas and the authority paid the fares for any Southborough child travelling over three miles to any borough school. From the 23 schools, four 11 to 18, mixed, comprehensive schools were chosen for study.

Two of these were selected because they were close to one another and the differences between them offered an interesting situation in which to explore parents' views. Tower Bridge School was a popular, ex-grammar school, with a good reputation for academic standards as well as arts and music. The headmaster and several of the senior staff had been at the school since its grammar school days and it could still claim that the vast majority of its intake were first-choice applicants.

London Bridge School, its neighbour, was considerably less popular and in recent years its numbers had declined significantly. Although neither school had particularly smart buildings or surroundings, London Bridge School's immediate vicinity mainly comprised a run-down council estate. Furthermore the opening of a new Jewish school in its traditional catchment area had taken away a proportion of its more well-off families. This whole situation was exacerbated by an enthusiastic road-building scheme that somewhat isolated the school from the rest of the borough and a recent council report in the paper which had erroneously omitted to include the school in the list of those not to be closed.

The third school, Richmond Bridge, was an ex-secondary modern school, which, despite falling rolls in the borough and the close proximity of two prestigious single-sex ex-grammar schools, had apparently been increasing both in popularity and in pupil numbers. For this reason alone it was decided to include it in the study.

The fourth school, All Saints' Roman Catholic, was chosen primarily because it was a Roman Catholic School with a liberal philosophy and it was felt that the views and considerations of Roman Catholic parents might differ from other parents. This school was popular, and its fully Roman Catholic intake consisted almost entirely of first-choice applicants. As it was a voluntary-aided school the governors had the right to decide upon the pupils to be admitted. Their criteria for admissions were reported to be (a) that the parents were practising Catholics and (b) proximity. The buildings and facilities were very good and the school placed great emphasis on involving the local community.

In Southborough, unlike the other three LEAs, the parents received the questionnaire whilst their child was still at primary school. The project selected 22 primary schools which were geographically associated with the four case-study secondary schools. By doing this it was felt that the differences in the parents' perceptions of the four schools would be better contrasted than if only those in the four schools had been sampled.

Choice of Schools

All parents in Southborough LEA were invited to choose from any of the authority's schools. Parents could name as many schools as they wished, but every named school would be regarded by the LEA as an equal first choice. As one would expect in a system where all parents had to make an active choice, a high percentage of Southborough parents felt that they had had a choice. There is no apparent reason why slightly more parents from London Bridge School appeared to take this view: see Table 6.14.

Table 6.14: 'Do you feel you were offered a choice of schools for your child?'

	YES %	NO %	BLANK %	TOTAL N
London Bridge	94	4	2	47
All Saints' R.C.	88	2	10	42
Tower Bridge	84	11	5	76
Richmond Bridge	83	15	2	47

It was of interest to the project to find out whether any parents actually wanted a particular school which they did not ask for, and if so, why this was the case. Their responses to this question indicated that although the vast majority of parents requested their preferred school, some 9 per cent overall did not (see Table 6.15). Tower Bridge School's parents were most notable in this with 16 per cent (12) not asking for their preferred school. When these parents were asked why they had done this five said the preferred school was too far away to travel, two of them said they would not have got in due to pressure for places from parents living nearer the school and another two said that they would have preferred a selective school but were doubtful if their children would have stood up to the academic pressure even if they had passed the entrance exam. Even though these figures reveal the views of only a very small number of parents, they do suggest that in an apparently free choice situation, some parents may still feel that they did not have a realistic choice. Those parents who commented that their preferred school would be full with those living nearer the school, raise a point which has already been discussed in Chapter 3: namely that the use of proximity as a criterion in popular schools is likely to create a type of catchment area.

Table 6.15: **'Was there a school you wanted your child to go to but did not ask for?'**

	YES	NO	BLANK	TOTAL
	%	%	%	%
London Bridge	6	87	7	100
All Saints' R.C.	10	88	2	100
Tower Bridge	16	75	9	100
Richmond Bridge	4	94	2	100

The vast majority of Southborough parents (62 per cent) commented that they had known what school they wanted before their child's last year in primary school. However it is interesting that whilst two of the schools should have similar results (London Bridge 60 per cent and Tower Bridge 62 per cent) there should be a large difference between All Saints' R.C. (71 per cent) and Richmond Bridge (53 per cent). It is possible that it is the Roman Catholic connection that is in operation here and presumably the increasing roll and popularity of Richmond Bridge explains parents changing their minds and/or finding places available here when other schools were full.

Reasons for Choosing Schools

Table 6.16 shows the first five aspects which were important to parents from each school when making their choices. Parents from the three non-denominational schools most commonly mentioned proximity to the school. This is quite a change from the pattern in the previous three LEAs, but may be due to the fact that the parents in the sample had children in primary schools which were local to the case study comprehensives.

Table 6.16: The first five aspects which were most important to Southborough parents when choosing a school (A more complete list is available – see Appendix 3.1)

%	London Bridge	All Saints' RC	Tower Bridge	Richmond Bridge
55		denominational		
50	proximity			
45		discipline		proximity
40	access/travel			
35		academic record	proximity	
30	academic record		academic record access/travel	facilities
25	facilities	access/travel	good school	academic record
20		co-educational		discipline wide subject choice co-educational
15	sibling connection		facilities	

The Roman Catholic School is perhaps most striking in its differences from the other three. Apart from a very strong denominational preference (55 per cent), there was also a major emphasis on 'discipline' (45 per cent). The significance of 'co-educational' at 19 per cent presumably reflects that while this is one of several Roman Catholic schools in the area, it is the only mixed one.

Surprisingly, Tower Bridge, the ex-grammar school, does not follow the academic pattern of the grammar schools seen elsewhere, but then, with the presence of two girls' grammar schools in the borough and several boys' independent schools in the vicinity, it may be that the ex-grammar status is no longer significant.

The parents' response to facilities is curious. Of the three non-denominational schools Richmond Bridge certainly has the better grounds and buildings, and this appears to be reflected in parents' responses. However, in terms of libraries, drama halls and so on the Roman Catholic School is also very well equipped, yet its parents did not respond to this in terms of reasons for choosing a school.

Influences on Parents' Choices and Their Use of School Information

THE CHILD

When parents were asked whether their child had had strong views about which school he or she attended, unlike in the other LEAs, in Southborough the variation between schools was small, between 68 and 83 per cent. The majority of parents felt that their child had had strong views about which school they were to go to.

WHO PARENTS TALKED TO ABOUT THE CHOICE OF SCHOOL

In choosing a school, Southborough parents were faced with a real choice which might suggest that they would want to hold lots of discussions about the various issues. At the same time however they were able to visit all the schools and brochures were readily available, a trend which might reduce the necessity for so many discussions. The overall pattern of who they talked to does not seem to be influenced by the amount of choice perceived at the different schools nor particularly by the type of school involved. Instead it seems more likely that there is a general pattern with individual differences due to heads' different procedures, e.g. the low percentage of London Bridge parents meeting junior school teachers is likely to reflect the junior school's particular administration in the same way as the individual heads of Richmond Bridge and All Saints' Schools seem to make themselves less accessible to prospective parents. If there is a slight trend it seems to be in the Roman Catholic School where a greater proportion of parents' discussions were held with teachers and heads than with other parents, friends and family, i.e. 56 per cent of All Saints' parents discussed the choice of school with professionals compared with an average of 41 per cent in the other schools (see Appendix: Table 6.2).

SCHOOL VISITS/TALKS

In Southborough LEA, every secondary school held a parents' evening, prior to choice for *any* parents who wished to attend. The dates of these were coordinated by the LEA so that they did not overlap, and they were published in the LEA booklet which all parents received via the primary school. The differences between the various groups of parents are not particularly significant save for the fact that the Roman Catholic parents seem to have adopted a slightly different pattern. More of All Saints' parents attended their own school's parents' evening than was observed at other schools: 81 per cent compared with 75 per cent on average. But All Saints' parents did not visit more schools in total than other parents and hence we may suppose that they were more specific in visiting just the one school (see Table 6.17).

As with other sources of information in Southborough, attendance at parents' evenings does not seem to correspond with the different amounts of perceived choice from school to school, but then the average number of schools visited by Southborough parents is already considerably higher than in the other authorities surveyed. It has already been noted that the information 'used' by Southborough parents as a whole was much more than in other LEAs, but this still did not prevent the small number of potential grammar school parents included in our survey of primary school parents from attending roughly twice as many visits and seeing twice as many brochures as other parents. (These grammar school parents visited, on average, 2.4 schools each compared with 1.5 schools for other parents.) It could be argued though that the increase was due to the uncertainty of securing a selective place and so another school had to be sought and visited just in case.

Table 6.17: 'How many parents' evenings did you attend before choice?'

	London Bridge	Tower Bridge	All Saints'	Richmond Bridge
	%	%	%	%
None	38	32	24	36
one	28	26	45	21
two	15	17	24	38
three or more	13	21	15	4
attended at least one	56	64	74	63

Southborough LEA asked its *primary* schools to hold general talks about transfer to secondary school prior to parents having to express a preference. Overall, approximately 80 per cent of Southborough parents said they were invited and 70 per cent attended such talks although both figures were considerably lower for London Bridge School (49 and 38 per cent respectively). These figures show quite clearly that parents do respond when invited. There was, of course, variation in the 'practical effectiveness' of individual primary schools' invitations. In four of the 22 primary schools, only 35 per cent or fewer parents reported being invited and not surprisingly their attendance rates were substantially lower than in other schools. It is this primary school effect that is visible when the parents are grouped by secondary school.

SCHOOL BROCHURES AND EXAMINATION RESULTS

The distribution of brochures and examination results at open evenings certainly provides the most effective method seen in the four LEAs and seemingly encourages very little variation between schools. However, there is still a sizeable minority of parents who do not attend open evenings and thus see no brochures or exam results.

In commenting about the brochure distribution some parents mentioned that they would like to have seen the brochures before the visits. To some extent the authority had met this demand by providing a page for each school in the LEA booklet, and of course, brochures were still available from the secondary schools after the open evenings if parents requested. However, in view of the authority's commitment to informed choice it might increase the brochures' readership if they were available from the primary schools throughout the period of choice – a practice we found generally to be shunned. (See Appendix: Tables 6.4 and 6.5.)

Summary

In Southborough, unlike the other three LEAs, it was not possible to detect any obvious links, by schools, between the amount of choice parents perceived they had and the different ways they reacted to choosing. This may well be because the level of perceived choice was uniformly high. Furthermore, because the LEA required all its schools to hold parents' evenings and make brochures and exam results available at these occasions, the variations in the parents' responses were again small. Thus, despite the fact that contrasting schools were chosen for this survey little variation was evident. Only the Roman Catholic School parents showed any real indications of behaving differently and having different priorities from parents in the non-denominational comprehensive schools. More of them had known which school they wanted for over a year, they were more specific in attending open evenings, and they appeared to have quite different concerns when choosing a school: proximity to the school was the most commonly mentioned aspect by parents from the other three schools, whilst Roman Catholic School parents were mostly concerned with denominational matters, followed by good discipline – a feature which appeared to interest the other sets of parents very little. Interestingly the Roman Catholic School parents also seemed to turn proportionately more to people in authority when discussing choice of school than did the other parents. In all it would be difficult from these results to find much reinforcement for the school descriptions given earlier in this section. The ranging descriptions of popularity, previous selective status, local competition and quality of buildings did not appear in parents' responses, and it may well be that in authorities where choice is taken very seriously parents operate on very different and more complex levels which as yet are not perceived by the LEA officers.

Conclusion

The parents' questionnaire set out to investigate parental response to LEA and school implementation of the 1980 Act. The design of the sample framework to include all the new parents in each case study school in four LEAs with different systems and allocations procedures, was intended to investigate the influence exerted by three separate aspects – family circumstances, LEA practices and school differences. This chapter has considered parents' reactions to the school differences, i.e. to the influences of the various schools' images and procedures. These schools were not in any way chosen to be a representative cross-section of schools and no attempt has been made to extrapolate to the national context. However they have served to indicate that to a large extent parents were influenced by more localized issues than might otherwise have been thought. Furthermore there was little evidence to suggest that even within the LEA all parents wanted the same from their child's school; indeed it was often apparent that the parents from different schools had varying views on what was important to them when choosing a school though the patterns here were not always very clear.

Whilst these differences were sometimes difficult to explain, they could often be seen to reflect the image that the school had been aiming to communicate. For example, in Shiretown LEA the community school's parents more frequently mentioned the child's welfare and happiness, whilst noticeably more of Oaklands School's parents mentioned that good discipline was important, and many more of Hollybush's parents commented on the school's good reputation. It was also found that proportionately few grammar school parents in Northtown and Seatown visited the school prior to choice. Perhaps the status of such schools was sufficient to reassure parents, or perhaps their priorities were linked to academic considerations rather than such factors as facilities and staff. This possibility seems to be reinforced by parents' responses from the grammar or more prestigious and popular comprehensive schools, in that they generally showed a greater concern for academic achievement of a school and a more active approach in gathering written information and exam results for more than one school.

With the publication of school information, it was often shown that where a school had actually sent out information or made it available at open evenings, there was a considerable take-up among its parents, as seen for example in Riverview School in Northtown LEA and Roseview School in Shiretown LEA. Also, where the published examination results were presented in brochures, there was a tendency for more parents to read these results than where results were published separately. Similarly with open evenings or heads' talks; where these were held and parents were invited, then parents attended. What is interesting here is that the tendency of parents to take an interest in their children's education by attending meetings and reading brochures gives the lie to the idea that parents are apathetic and cannot be encouraged to participate. Of course, having a degree of choice would also help.

When looking at the amount of choice parents perceived that they had been offered, it was most noticeable that where parents felt that there was little or no choice, fewer of their children felt strongly about the school they were to attend and fewer parents took up opportunities to discuss the choice with other people. Also it seems that many more parents in grammar schools and prestigious comprehensive schools had actually expressed a preference for the school, rather than accepting the one that the authority first offered. It seems reasonable to assume that this is linked to the greater activity these parents demonstrated in seeking out written information from more than one school and in visiting two or more possible alternative schools.

One final point emerged which seems to have important ramifications for LEAs considering the processes by which parents are offered a preference. In Northtown a very high percentage of parents from the two town secondary modern schools said that they felt that they had been offered a choice. Indeed as large a proportion of parents in these two schools felt they had been given a choice as did parents from Southborough, the optimal choice LEA. This clearly suggests that the act of filling in a form stating a preference, regardless of whether the choice is between similar or different schools, is sufficient to give the feeling of having been offered a choice. However, two questions still remain: first, how schools create a sense of commitment and belonging where pupils and parents feel they have had no choice whatever, and secondly, whether the choice between like schools is as likely to enhance parents' feelings of a real choice and hence commitment to a school as might a choice between diverse schools.

CHAPTER 7

What Happens When the LEA Says 'No'?

Introduction

For many years it has been recognized that the principles of 'parental choice' and 'efficient management of schools' will often result in a conflict of interests. Quite simply, the parents' reasons for choosing schools can be based upon different premises from those used by LEAs in fulfilling their management role. In the majority of cases the parents' choices can be accommodated within the LEA's system, but this still leaves approximately 8 to 9 per cent of parents who do not get their first preference (see Appendix: Table 7.1). In essence, a conflict arises between the wishes of the individual and the decisions of the LEA in the exercise of its responsibility for providing education for all. This chapter explores the institutionalized processes set up to resolve these conflicts and, since most of these processes are designed to operate at the individual case level, the chapter will primarily concentrate on this facet of their operation. The resolution of individual conflicts has, however, been argued to influence LEAs' overall procedures for all parents in subsequent years (see Chapter 2) and this issue, along with an evaluation of the whole functioning of educational appeals, will be taken up in the conclusion.

The Information for Parental Choice Project did not initially set out to study school admission appeals. The appeals were thought to concern too few people to be of interest to the majority, and furthermore, the activities of no more than 2 per cent of parents were not thought to bear upon the remaining 98 per cent. However, as the research progressed it became apparent that the appeals occupied a considerable amount of LEA time and thinking, and that their final impact seemed proportionately more important than the statistics alone would suggest. As such, the institutionalized processes of allowing parents to appeal against the LEA's allocation decisions were described by a number of education officers as exerting a considerable influence over the whole exercise of parental choice.

In recognizing this, the project sought to find out more about the appeals, and although it was not possible to attend any hearings, information was collected by means of a questionnaire to all LEAs and from interviews with 45 education officers in England and Wales. Comments were also received from a small number of parents who had appealed against their LEA's decisions, but the number was too small to allow any generalization.

Unless otherwise stated, the views and comments expressed relate to admissions to secondary schools in September 1984 and basically refer to the third 'round' of statutory appeals since 1982. The timing of the research is significant in that it falls between two important procedural innovations. The first, a judicial review of a statutory appeal took place in May 1984 and suggested the need for major changes in the way education appeal committees interpreted cases and in the way that evidence was presented.* In the following year, in February 1985, the local authority associations (ACC and AMA), in consultation with the Council on Tribunals, presented a new set of guidelines with a number of amendments including some which reflected the recommendations of the High Court case (ACC, 1985). Thus at the time of responding to our questions most LEAs were aware of the South Glamorgan judgement but had not then changed their own systems. One interesting possibility was that the changing nature of the statutory appeals might be further readjusting the position of the parent/LEA balance since its 'setting' in 1980.

From Choice to Appeal

There is no point in appealing if the authority has offered a place at the chosen school. From the LEA questionnaire returns it was apparent that just over 91 per cent of parents were offered the school they 'wanted' at the initial allocation. For this chapter the

---

* R. v. *South Glamorgan Appeals Committee, ex parte Dafydd Evans* – referred to as the South Glamorgan High Court Case – 10th May 1984.

interest lies with the 8+ per cent who were 'unhappy' at this stage. In the 'free choice' areas (as described in Chapter 3) approximately 8 per cent of parents' first choices were not accepted by their LEAs and in the catchment-area authorities roughly the same proportion of parents wrote back rejecting the school offered and asking for another. Of these 8 per cent in catchment areas, some will have had their request granted straight away and hence the figure will be somewhat lower than that of free choice areas (see Appendix: Table 7.1).

Once the authority actually said 'No' to the parent's choice, and overall a fair estimate might be in the region of 7 per cent of cases, then various negotiation, discussion and review processes were often enacted. At the end of this period the parents could ask for a statutory appeal if they wished and 1.3 per cent and 1.2 per cent did so in 1983 and 1984 respectively (see Table 7.1). Thus, approximately 5 per cent of the parents had their initial choice rejected but did not take up their right of a statutory appeal. Some of these parents will have gained their choice during this period of negotiation whilst others will have changed their minds or given up.

To some extent a number of authorities have regarded the education appeal committees as coming at the end of their review procedures, and indeed some felt them to be totally unnecessary as they believed their review procedures were satisfactory. But the review bodies, as opposed to the statutory education appeal committees were, and are, LEA committees. In one LEA, apart from discussions with an education officer, the parent's cases were reviewed three times before the parent could resort to a statutory appeal. In several other LEAs there were two-stage reviews. Typically, if the parent rejected the LEA's choice there was an interview with an area or assistant education officer to explore the ground, and this was often followed by a local LEA review to ensure that the published criteria had been correctly applied. The next stage brought in the chief education officer, or his deputy, and finally, the elected members considered the arguments. All this occurred before the statutory appeal was called, and apart from the interview with the AEO, the other review stages were all completed in the absence of the parents with any arguments being submitted in writing.

Some authorities also operated explicit waiting lists which the parents were told of, whilst others simply kept unpublicized lists of

Table 7.1: **Numbers and percentages of statutory appeals for secondary admission in England and Wales***

	1983	1984
% of stat. appeals in free choice areas[1]	1.9% (N=2786)	1.5% (N=2035)
% of stat. appeals in catchment areas[1]	0.9% (N=2688)	1.0% (N=2496)
Overall % of stat. appeals	1.3%	1.2%
TOTAL number of stat. appeals reported[2]	5474	4531
Overall % of stat. appeals decided in favour of LEA[3]	57.5%	57.4%

Notes

*   All these figures should exclude primary, middle and VA appeals as well as casual transfer appeals occurring during the school year.

1   The percentage is calculated from the number of pupils in that cohort – see Appendix: Table 7.1.

2   This is thought to represent about 63% of the secondary appeals for England and Wales.

3   This percentage is calculated from the total number of appeals reported to us.

the unsuccessful applicants, in order of priority, so they could be notified if a place became available.

From the interviews with the LEAs it was possible to summarize the various reasons for the variety of procedures described above. The initial interviews between the parents and education officers seemed to serve at least three legitimate functions:

a   the parent could explain his or her reasons in full and the officer could thus reassess the status of the parent's case against the published criteria, e.g. apparently many parents fail to state the sibling connection or medical reason on the application forms;

b   the officer could explain the authority's position, the system of reviews, the method of appealing, and how the waiting list worked;

c   the officer could talk about the other schools and seek to find an acceptable alternative for the parent.

It is notable that all these functions operated within the published admissions procedures. There have been instances, though, where these interviews have been described by the officers as 'negotiations' and 'deals', and here it would seem that the criteria were reinterpreted or that the definition of 'full' was changed. In one LEA the review panel was a sub-committee of the education committee and explicitly in its brief was the right to override its own intended intake limits. This would seem specifically to favour those parents who ask for a review.

It is generally assumed that no child will be refused admission to a school if that school is not full, providing of course that neither selection nor denominational factors are upset by that child's admission. However this was not always the case. In some catchment-area authorities, admissions officers refused out-catchment-area parents their choices where the number of applicants from outside the catchment area exceeded the number of spare places left when the catchment-area pupils had been allocated. In effect some parents were refused before the normal grounds for refusal applied. Not all those parents receiving a notice of refusal would have subsequently argued their case, and hence this approach tended to offer greater success to those who argued their case and who went to review or appeal.

Returning to the more usual procedures, if the LEA has stated that the school is full and the parents' reasons have been closely checked against the published criteria, then once there has been an informal interview it is debatable what an LEA review can achieve apart from convincing parents that their case is lost. One LEA claimed its review bodies reinterpreted the criteria and indeed it was argued in this LEA that its criteria for deciding whether or not to accept a child should more properly be considered as 'factors to take into account'. But this means that the LEA itself was inconsistent in its dealings with parents and that once more those who did not seek a review received different and probably less favourable treatment.

Other LEAs argued that the review could ensure that any casual vacancies that occurred during this period could be properly filled, but there again this favoured those who sought a review as opposed to those who simply stayed on the waiting list. The waiting list is not without opponents. Some authorities refused to operate waiting lists as they believed them to be unsettling for the children. In stable, rural catchment-area authorities the number of casual vacancies that might occur during the run-up to starting the secondary school could be few and the waiting list may well frustrate more than it satisfies. However, in urban areas many more vacancies are likely to arise and its value becomes more apparent.

One unusual approach arose where an LEA used waiting lists but changed the criteria for determining the parents' place on the list once the closing date had passed. Before the closing date the LEA's normal criteria were applied in determining the priority for each case, but afterwards parents were simply added in the order in which they applied.

The waiting list, whether publicized or otherwise, creates a further problem for LEAs during the run-up to the statutory appeals. Some authorities we talked to 'froze' the allocations procedures at an early date and effectively left the statutory education appeals committee with the decision of how to fill casual vacancies that arose during the interim. The education appeals committees were thus given some room to manoeuvre, something a number of them had asked of their LEAs, and they could guarantee to accede to some parents' cases, but they could only fill the places from the pool of appellants. The opposite approach was reported in an item on the agenda of one LEA's schools' sub-committee meeting:

> This year, however, certain Appeal Committees and Appeal Committee Chairmen have objected to this approach [of freezing waiting lists pending the outcome of the statutory appeals], and have felt it to be unfair that appeal outcomes should impact on those pupils on waiting lists and whose parents have chosen not to appeal.

Three years earlier this very point had been raised during the discussions of the 1979 Bill by Andrew Bennett, M.P., who asked:

> What happens when the matter goes to Appeal? If the Appeals Committee turn everybody down because the school is already full, everyone will feel that the Appeals Committee is a farce.

The one possibility is that the local authority cheats from the start by not making all the places available initially but keeping a few in its back pocket available for the Appeals Committee to allocate. Having gone through all this rigmarole children will win their appeal as it were, only by getting the place that would have been available anyway if there had been no Appeals procedure.

Bennett; House of Commons Debate,
Standing Ctte. D., Col. 577,
11th Dec. 1979

The authority whose agenda is referred to above recognized these points and argued that the waiting lists are part of their proper admissions procedures and hence that they should always apply up to the carefully worked out intake limits. Any child allocated by the education appeal committees should be considered an exception and thus be considered to be beyond the intake number and thus not reduce the access of parents who do not appeal.

It is within this approach that we see what is possibly the fairest system. The LEA publishes its admissions procedures and expected intake figures and then operates solely on that basis: it sets out to fill its schools according to its published criteria. There is no room within this system for negotiation, deals or saved places, though the LEA would encourage the parents to meet the education officer to discuss the issues. By removing 'reinterpretation' and the late adjustment of intake figures, the LEA avoids favouring the more argumentative parents at the expense of those who believe the LEA to have given them a complete and final decision the first time round. During the course of the research the project team encountered several authorities which held no reviews or informal appeals before the statutory appeal stage was reached.

It has been argued, however (Dr Boyson, House of Commons, 20th Dec. 82) that the 'informal' LEA reviews can be useful in identifying and acceding to the potentially successful appeals before they reach the statutory stage, an effect which would save time and also reduce the number of appeals which go against the LEA. Furthermore, the new Guidelines recommend the use of 'informal procedures with a view to encouraging settlement of admissions decisions without the need for an appeal under the Act' (ACC, 1985). In discussing this with authorities the position has been described where the informal appeals have removed the 'need' for any statutory appeals to arise by finally acceding to every request that stayed the course. But where the LEA accedes to all or most of its parental requests at the review stage, and this assumes it has already checked that it has applied its criteria correctly, then it must increase the possibility that it is favouring the small vocal group by changing the ground rules at this late stage and by allowing the process of attrition to whittle away their competition.

The Statutory Appeals: Procedures and Administration

The rationale for setting up statutory local appeals under the 1980 Education Act was described in Chapter 2 but little space was given to the procedural details. The Act gave new rights to parents and laid down specific obligations for LEAs to meet. Under section 7(1), it was required that every LEA should make arrangements for enabling the parent of a child to appeal against –

(a)   any decision made by or on behalf of the authority as to the school at which education is to be provided for the child in the exercise of the authority's functions;* and

(b)   any decision made by or on behalf of the governors of a county or controlled school maintained by the authority refusing the child admission to such a school.*

Furthermore, under section 7(5) –

The decision of an appeal committee on any such appeal shall be binding on the local education authority or governors by or on whose behalf the decision under appeal was made and, in the case of a decision made by or on behalf of a local education

---

* Para. (a) is an appeal against the school the LEA has chosen. Para. (b) is an appeal against the refusal to admit the child to the school chosen by the parents. Some bodies interpret (a) to apply to LEAs and thus (b) to the voluntary sector – see the new Guidelines, paragraph 7J (ACC, 1985), whilst others interpret both (a) and (b) as applying to LEAs and quite reasonably argue that the voluntary sector would only become involved with (b) as voluntary-aided schools do not 'suggest' schools or 'place' pupils. The latter interpretation is adopted in this report.

authority, on the governors of any county or controlled school at which the committee determines that a place should be offered to the child in question.

[The full version of section 7 appears in Appendix 2.2.]

With such powers the committees need to be carefully set up and managed. Schedule 2 to the 1980 Act entered into considerable detail and it is possible to take the specific features and see what has happened in practice.

The Composition of Education Appeal Committees

Part 1 of Schedule 2 to the Act states that the appeal committees shall consist of three, five or seven members. It was left to the LEA's discretion to decide the number. Only two of the authorities interviewed had chosen seven-member committees, and one of these authorities had had no appeals up to the summer of 1984. Several education officers commented that five was an easier number to manage and that seven was too big. A number also reflected that three was too small to give good advice to the chairman. In all just about half of the authorities interviewed had adopted committees of five. Many claimed that five had a further advantage in that if one member could not attend, and if all parties agreed, the appeal could continue by the simple expedient of shedding another member and reconvening as a three-member committee. Some authorities however expressed the view that they could not find enough people to serve on five-member committees to start with, and that three was the only practical response.

In choosing who can serve on these appeal committees the Act is again specific. The LEA is given a majority of no more than one and the chairman shall not be a member of the education committee although he or she may still be a member of the authority. The chairman has a second, or casting, vote if necessary. The other person(s) are expected to be knowledgeable about local education and are typically teachers, retired heads or parents. None of the committee members should have been involved in any part of the decision making which resulted in the appeal being lodged and nor should they have any vested interest in its outcome (Schedule 2, 1980 Act). By creating a panel of potential committee members the

LEA should be able to select each committee's membership to avoid these troubles.

A further person is required to be the clerk to the committee – an administrative post with responsibility for supplying the necessary staff, for allocating appeals to appeal committees, and for ordering the business. The clerk also has the role of offering advice on procedure or law, of assisting the committee by reference to notes of evidence and also of recording the committee's decisions and reasons (ACC, 1985). The role of the clerk as described here does not come directly from the Act but from the guidelines drawn up following discussions between the local authority associations and the Council on Tribunals in 1981. In this respect the Council on Tribunals has been given a supervisory role in the Act and is charged with overseeing the statutory appeals.

These Guidelines make similar requirements of impartiality for the clerk as the Act makes for the committee members. They say that the clerk to the committee

. . . should be seen as an independent source of advice on procedure. He or she should not be an employee who in the course of his employment by the authority or the school or schools concerned deals with the admission of children to schools.

ACC, 1985

Between the Act and the Guidelines we can see 'the setting up of an appeal committee which acts independently of those people who took the original decision' (Boyson, House of Commons Debate; Col. 805; 20th Dec. 1982). (It is interesting to note the use of the word 'independent' here: in earlier usage it was taken to imply that the appeals committee was independent of the authority. Here, within the authority's structure, the committee is just independent of one group of people.)

The appointment of the appeal committee members by the local authority and the allowance of an LEA majority on the committees raises questions of whether or not appeal committees will be neutral towards the LEA's policy. When the project asked education officers about who were actually appointed to these committees we were, for the most part, quoted 'chapter and verse' of the Act. The question was perhaps inappropriate for many since the appointment to the committees was more often dealt with the chief executive's office than by members of the education department. However one or two of the replies were quite revealing. In one authority the three-person appeals committee comprised the chairman and vice-chairman of the education committee and a retired headteacher who thus chaired the appeals committee. The LEA's case at the statutory appeal was always handled by the Director of Education. Whilst this appears perfectly legal, the committee's independence does seem very questionable.

The issue of the appeals committees' independence has also arisen in a broader sense in terms of the committees' affiliations and support, not only for the authority per se, but also for the political party which has the majority on the council and for its ideals. In 1983, Mr Yardley, for the Commission for Local Administration in England, the Local Ombudsman, found that 'maladministration causing injustice' had occurred in one LEA where it was felt that the 'appeal committees were likely to be biased in favour of the Council' (Investigation into Complaints 312 *et al.,* 8th Dec. 1983). In a situation described to the project a five-person appeals committee was considering several similar appeals to one primary school over two days. The appeals committee membership reflected the council's two-party composition. On the first day when all members were present the parents lost their appeals. On the second day two majority-party committee members could not attend and so a three-person committee was convened with the 'minority party' in the majority. The parents won their cases on the second day. In all likelihood both committees made good and proper decisions according to their separate standpoints, but the evident strength of these standpoints would seem to deny the committee any independence.

A similar difficulty arises with the clerks to the appeals committees. If the parents are to be present when all the evidence is submitted, and no fresh evidence or interpretation is to be offered in their absence, then it seems important that the clerk, who stays with the committee when they deliberate, should be absolutely independent. At least one authority advertized for clerks in the local papers and created part-time jobs for people with no other LEA connection. In other instances clerks were brought in from other departments in the authority, a move that might normally avoid problems except where the clerk, as a legal adviser, might already be advising the education department as happens in at least one authority. There were also clerks who were intimately involved with planning the intake numbers and others who although not directly concerned with admissions might have worked for those who were, e.g. in one LEA the clerk to the appeals was the area education officer's secretary.

Many of these issues arose out of expediency. The government provided no additional resources for these appeals and so many LEAs looked to their existing staff before making new appointments. Similarly, there was, and is, a finite pool of people who can sit on day-time committees and act as appeal committee members. As a result, in some cases financial and managerial expediency resulted in less than ideal practice.

One example of this can be seen in the sensitive role of the clerk in the job of appointing committees and allocating appeals to appeals committees. In one instance this was taken to mean appointing committee members from the panel who were appropriate to, or who could match, the parents. If the parents were using a barrister then a member of the committee would be drawn from the same profession and so forth. The concept of an independent appeals committee seems to disappear when the procedures are manipulated on this basis, and yet it seems most reasonable that lay people should not be confronted by people trained in argument. The alternative approach, as suggested in the 1985 Guidelines (ACC, 1985), is to allow the LEA to be legally represented when the parents are, and this would not affect the composition of the committee. This seems to offer fair redress to the LEA whilst still maintaining the appeal committee's independence. The business of matching appeal committees to parents seems fraught with problems.

The selection of members to committees also serves to ensure that clashes of interest can be avoided. An LEA might require for instance that teacher members should not sit on committees and hear cases relating to neighbouring or competing schools to the one where they work – the law already stops them hearing cases for their own school. Many LEAs told us that their solution to this was for members to serve in different towns or divisions from their own.

The Training of Committee Members

The idea of the committees being knowledgeable raises the question of training. Again the project encountered a large degree of variation between the authorities. Some have given no training at all to their committees and at least one officer has argued that any training would risk the charge of biasing the members. In addition, some appeals committees are reported as having said that they did not want any anyway. Most LEAs, however, seem to have given a briefing session in 1982 but only a few have followed this up with any subsequent seminars or lectures. It is assumed, of course, that all appeals committee members receive the Guidelines.

Without training sessions or Guidelines it would be difficult to see how an appeals committee might evolve over the years, and yet, as described at the beginning of this chapter, there have been some very significant changes in how the committees have been expected to carry out their function. Initially, in 1982 they were perceived as extensions of the LEA which would not question the LEA's case, but more recently there has been a move towards greater independence. Whilst the causes for this change will be discussed in the next section of this chapter, the concern here is the question of how these geographically isolated and part-time committees which only meet for a few days per year can keep abreast of national changes.

Final Dates and Other Restrictions

In writing the 1980 Act the government was aware of the pressures upon authorities that arise from inter-sector transfer and choice of schools. Thus, whilst giving the parents the right to appeal against allocation decisions the government required the appeals to fit into the arrangements made by the authority (Schedule 2, para. 11, 1980 Education Act – see Appendix 2.4). This has led to some confusion relating to the timing of appeals and to the possibility of a parent reappealing at frequent intervals.

Many authorities told parents that there was a last date for lodging an appeal in the normal year of transfer, and administratively this makes a good deal of sense. A number of other authorities required the parents to request the appeal within a certain number of days of being told the authority's final decision: typically they gave 14 or 21 days (the Guidelines suggest 14) although at least one authority gave 28 days. But having given a deadline in one form or another, only three out of the 45 officers interviewed thought they would enforce this date and a number of authorities suggested that it would be illegal to do so.

Part of the problem seems to stem from the wording of the Act. Section 7(1) specifically states:

> Every local education authority shall make arrangements for enabling the parent of a child to appeal against –

> (a)   any decision made by or on behalf of the authority as to the school at which education is to be provided for the child in the exercise of the authority's functions; and

> (b)   any decision made by or on behalf of the governors of a county or controlled school maintained by the authority refusing the child admission to such a school.

If a parent is refused the right to appeal on the grounds of being out of time, then the authority does not seem to be making the sort of arrangements for enabling an appeal to take place as are specified here.

So far this issue has related to administrative grounds only. However, one authority decided that once the appeals had started that was the time to stop any more being filed. Their argument was that when the non-appealing parents heard the outcome of the appeals they too would want an appeal, a situation that would (a) make the appeals drag on inordinately and (b) present problems for the education appeals committees as they would not be able to hear all the cases for any one school before reaching a decision.

In a very small number of instances, LEAs applied other restrictions to the right of appeal. One authority considered 11+ selection to be outside the allocation procedures – a stance that is not endorsed by the Local Ombudsman; another would not allow an appeal until the three internal reviews had been completed, and a third told parents that they could not appeal against being given a school they had listed as one of their 'equal' choices – a statement that directly contradicts the parent's right to appeal against any

LEA allocation decision, even if it means that the parent is not exactly being sensible.

One authority claimed that because the parents could appeal again the next term if they wanted, there was no point in stopping any appeal at this stage. The procedures for reappealing seem very unclear, but as any parent may use the Act to seek a 'casual' transfer from one school to another at any time, and since all the same procedural rules still apply, it would seem that parents are fully entitled to do so. One authority described having a parent who had been appealing for three years now and two said they were seeking legal advice on the possibility of banning reappeals. A parent may appeal in connection with more than one school and for two possible reasons (see page 163) and it was reported that because of this there were parents in one authority with as many as three appeals running concurrently. The use of the appeal against the school chosen by the authority (type 'a') is apparently becoming much less frequent than the appeal against the refusal of the school the parents want (type 'b').

As a footnote to the use of the 1980 Act for casual transfers, which bring about appeals on a weekly basis throughout the year in some LEAs, a number of comments were offered relating to the unfortunate use of this legislation by the less desirable elements to keep moving from one school to another. It was felt that some of these children moved on rather than taking criticism and possible punishment, and that the Act made it impossible for the receiving heads to refuse admission if their school was not full.

Multiple Appeals and Individual Independence

Some parents choose to have their cases heard together. Where, for instance, their argument might be the same and there might be little or no competition between them, these group appeals seem quite reasonable. The typical example of this would be with several parents from one small village all wanting to cross the catchment boundary and attend the geographically nearer school. However, where there is an element of competition between the parents, and this would seem to be fairly common since parents are normally appealing for a limited number of places (see Bull, 1980 and 1985), then individual hearings and decisions might be more appropriate. The new Guidelines are quite specific on this:

Each decision on the allocation of school places will be based on the individual circumstances of each case and this principle must govern the conduct of each appeal.

(ACC, para. 10,a, 1985)

However, many education officers described instances where the committees would hear all the cases for each school before reaching any decisions and this reflects a later suggestion in the same Guidelines:

Injustice could result if the appeal of one parent at an oversubscribed school were to be decided before the appeal of another for the same school had been considered. Where it is not possible to hear all appeals in relation to one school at the same time, the appeal committee should therefore, if practicable adjourn its decisions in relation to that school until all have been heard, and then issue them.

(ACC, para. 7(i), 1985)

Whilst respecting the practical grounds for this latter approach, there does appear to be an inherent contradiction between it and the idea of each case being unaffected by any other. One LEA has considered the arguments and reached the following position:

In the guidance which has been issued to authorities jointly by the Council on Tribunals and the A.M.A., the option is specifically raised of arranging for all of the appeals relating to a particular school to be heard by a single committee which would make its decisions after all relevant appeals had been heard. Clearly this arrangement enables both a consistency of approach on the part of the appeal committee and a weighing of the relative merits of particular cases. Some authorities have adopted this approach; the attraction in our context would be clear with, for example, 20 appeals this year being concerned with one school. The argument against this approach, and in justification of our present arrangements, is the fundamental one of each case being heard and decided on its merits and not on the basis of comparative judgements.

In 1984, Mr Cook, a Local Ombudsman, took a slightly different line on this practice, and commented that:

> The practice when determining one appeal of taking into account information obtained in the course of hearing another appeal may well result in the Appeal Committee having a complete grasp of all the issues. But another result can be that the Appeal Committee are taking into account information unknown to an individual appellant, who is thus at the disadvantage that he or she cannot challenge that information. That appears *contrary to the principles of natural justice* and is a point which commands attention in future years.
>
> (Commission for Local Administration in England, Investigation into Complaints Nos 276, 332 and 435, 15th February 1985, York)

It does appear that the idea of each appeal being individually considered loses ground when they are not only competitive but also acknowledged to be so in the way the committees work. One authority, for instance, described its appeal committees as being more lenient when there was only a small number of appeals for any one school, whilst another actually thought its committee was acting illegally in hearing several cases before reaching a decision: an interpretation that arises from the South Glamorgan High Court Case (p.10, line D: see footnote on page 157). There seems to be no way out of this dilemma whilst appeal committees see themselves as part of the allocation procedures rather than, as was suggested earlier, the body that deals only with exceptions to the LEA's allocation procedure.

The Order of the Hearing

It seems as if, prior to 1984, most appeals committees required parents to establish their case before the LEA gave its reasons for refusing their application. The then current Guidelines endorsed this. However on 10th May 1984 the High Court judgement in South Glamorgan directed, amongst other things, that the authority must prove it has a case for refusing the parents' wishes before the parents have to establish their argument. Surprisingly, only a few

LEAs had implemented this directive in the summer of 1984 but one might expect it to become more common from 1985 onwards as it is clearly laid out in the new Guidelines, although only as a suggestion. This new order seems to fit well with, and indeed derive from, the sequencing of section 6 of the Act which requires the LEA to comply with the parent's preference except in certain circumstances. In other words, the strength of the parent's case is irrelevant if the LEA cannot give a good reason to refuse it.

The Cost of the Appeals

As a last procedural question the authorities were asked to estimate how much an average appeal cost in either time or money. Unfortunately no complete estimates were available. The problem lay with the majority of appeals being administered by the chief executive's department whilst the review procedures and the LEA's case preparation takes place in the education department. However a range of opinions was offered which varied from the unusual: 'Not very much now as we use the same arguments', to the more common: 'Consumes vast amounts of time and resources', and, 'Incredibly time consuming'.

In terms of education officer time the descriptions of cost varied from 5½ to 15 hours per case, this being the time taken from when the parents and LEA first disagreed until the outcome of the statutory appeal was known. Ten hours seemed a quite common estimate. In terms of money, one off-the-cuff estimate of £300 was given whilst another officer approximated his estimate to 'hundreds of pounds per appeal'. The chief executive's department in one LEA had calculated in minute detail that the administrative cost of each appeal was £139. This figure, however, excluded the education officer time. If there were 10,000 statutory appeals in England during 1983 then it is reasonable to assume that between 1½ and 2½ million pounds was spent on carrying out the appeals alone.

Statutory Appeals and the LEAs' Arguments

With the first statutory appeals in 1982 it appears that many committees were prepared to accept the authorities' word for a school being full: if a school had reached its expected intake or planned admissions target no one was going to question whether that target really meant the school was full or not. However, there are many ways to define 'full' and not all of them imply that the addition of one extra child would prejudice the efficient education of the others. With time, and especially after the South Glamorgan case, the strength of the intake number argument was reduced and more LEAs have moved directly to the prejudice argument.

In many ways this accords with the actual planning, staffing and management of schools. Authorities were asked whether they used the published intended intake numbers in calculating their staffing requirements. The majority replied that they did not, and of the remaining LEAs, none gave an unqualified 'Yes'. In essence staffing requirements were reported as being worked out on the number of pupils the LEA expected to go to the school. In some cases applications would match the published number, because the school would fill, but very often vacancies would remain. Where an LEA wished to cushion the effects of falling rolls they might staff the school according to its previous year's intake, and in a number of instances full or part curriculum-based staffing was also used, i.e. in determining a minimum number of staff the needs of the curriculum were taken into account so that the required breadth of curriculum was maintained. Many authorities said that they completed most of their allocation decisions before the final staffing estimates were made each year and thus the staffing was based on actual transfer numbers instead of guesses. The essential point in most of these situations was that the expected intake number per se was irrelevant to the resources argument.

The question then arises of whether it will cost the authority anything extra if one more child is put into a school. The LEAs were asked what they would do as regards staffing if an appeals committee, as opposed to the LEA itself, broached the intended intake figure. Well over half simply replied that no extra staffing would be provided and a further few said that nothing would be done for 12 months and only after that would the situation be assessed in the normal way. The remaining authorities said that they would provide staff subject to two conditions. Some said they would only bring in additional staff if they could remove them from elsewhere. In other words the LEA had a fixed pool of staff which could be divided in different ways, but not increased. The other qualification related to there being sufficient necessity, i.e. just exceeding the intended intake figure by one or two was not enough to justify extra staff, the numbers had to be quite large. In this respect most of those LEAs saying 'Yes' had not yet felt the need to provide extra staff.

A number of authorities were quite emphatic that if they were to increase the staff as a result of an appeal committee decision, they would defeat their own argument that additional admissions to a school would be prejudicing the education of others. However, some of these LEAs had not always applied this principle and extra staff had been brought in when the LEAs had felt that the education appeal committees' decisions would be too damaging if the ensuing staffing shortage were not rectified.

A very fundamental issue arises here from the criteria used by the appeal committees. The 1980 Act (Schedule 2, para. 7) requires the committees to include the following in their considerations:

(*a*) any preference expressed by the appellant in respect of the child as mentioned in section 6 of this Act; and

(*b*) the arrangements for the admission of pupils published by the local education authority or the governors under section 8 of this Act.

It has been suggested that initially, in 1982, the appeal committees were perhaps too accepting of the LEA's arrangements and that some committees did not consider it their role to challenge either the admissions criteria or the LEA's statement that a school was full. More recently, though, it appears that their decision making has broadened out, and, as one education officer adroitly commented, the only appeals he was now aware of were obviously against his LEA's criteria.

A number of education officers have commented that recent appeals have given more weight to social and emotional matters than to the observation of the LEA's procedures and school management requirements. One appeal committee in 1984 reported to its authority that:

They found the appeals very difficult to determine and only reached their decisions after much deliberation. They felt however that the Education Authority was better able to respond to the very real difficulties the Authority would face should certain appeals be allowed than the individual parents to the difficulties they would face should their appeals be unsuccessful.

Conclusion

The application of a statutory local appeals procedure to the LEAs' allocation procedures was new to the education system in 1982. Furthermore, for the Council on Tribunals, which has oversight of these appeals, the education appeal committees represented a considerable departure from their 50 or so other panels and tribunals. Primarily, in these appeals, there were no common ground rules for the committees in reaching their decisions and, what is more, in education, unlike the other appeals, many of the committees' decisions would be influenced by competitive aspects which arise from a plurality of appellants seeking very few places. Inevitably, then, to write a conclusion after only three years' practice is somewhat premature. However, when the substantial number of appeals is taken into account (approximately 8900 in 1982 and 10,000 in 1983 in England alone), and the importance of the committees' role in education is considered, there seems to be good reason to step back and contemplate the whole process in the light of the issues that have been raised by those involved.

Most of what has been described so far in this chapter relates to the problems and issues that have been commented upon by education officers in coming to grips with this new phenomenon. But some authorities have said that there were no problems, and at least one authority has expressed satisfaction with the statutory appeals on the grounds that they were easier to operate and fairer for parents than that LEA's previous system. However, the evidence does not seem to suggest a complete success story, and a very telling point was made in a report by the Commission for Local Administration in England in January 1984. Having reviewed some of the 80+ cases that had been referred to them between 1982 and 1984, they alluded to: 'the wider issue of whether some appeal committees know what their task is'. The point could also have been made about whether appeal committees have one or many tasks and, given the real constraints that LEAs are bound by, whether any of these tasks is really viable.

As mentioned in Chapter 2 the appeal committees were set up to do two things. The first was to decide between individual parents and the LEA within the local context, whilst still being independent of the LEA, and the second was to provide an independent control over the LEA's practices in order to protect the parents' interests as regards choosing schools. This latter function was seen to operate through the first, so that by controlling the number of parent successes, the appeal committees could influence the balance between the parents and the LEA.

The idea of arbitrating between the parents and the LEA is very complex. If the LEA has done its job properly there should be no places left in the schools according to the LEA's definition: how then can a committee ever satisfy a parent's appeal without challenging the LEA's arguments? Jack Tweedie (1986) has identified four approaches that appeal committees take in reaching their decisions.

1   *'The Policy Rights'* approach is solely concerned with whether the LEA has applied its own criteria correctly. Appeal judgements therefore reflect only the accuracy of the LEA's implementation.

2   *'The Substantial Justice'* approach takes greater account of the parents' individual circumstances and is prepared to bend the LEA's procedures to a small degree but only if in doing so it will not substantially affect the outcome of the LEA's allocation programme and policy.

3   *'The Individualist Rights'* approach focuses exclusively on the individual parents' request without regard for general policy concerns or numbers of other parents who are also appealing. This approach also assumes that the parents' case is good unless the LEA can establish that the admission of just one extra child into the school would result in greater harm than the benefit accrued from admitting the child.

4   *'The Administrative Justice'* approach requires the committee to make an independent determination of whether the LEA policy is justified in terms of the collective goals and consequences that the LEA must take

into account. The parents' case is automatically granted if the committee finds the LEA's policy unjustified. If the policy is found to be justified then the committee moves on to question whether the parents' case justifies an exemption to that policy.

Before giving further consideration to these four approaches it is as well to consider their context. Some appeal committees regard themselves as part of the allocation procedures, i.e. they asked for places to be left for their disposal, whereas some LEAs regard the appeals as being beyond the allocation procedures (see page 162). Furthermore some appeals can be considered on an individual basis, where perhaps only one child is trying to enter a ten-form entry school, compared with the competitive factors that apply when perhaps 20 children are applying for a three-form entry school. Underlying all this is the LEA's need to run an efficient education service at a time of severe economic constraint.

Consideration of the tenets of natural justice and of the rights of those who do not appeal would suggest that a strong case can be made for each appeal to be adjudicated on a individual basis and for educational appeal committees to be no part of the LEA's allocation procedure, i.e. the role of the committees is to adjudicate after the LEA allocation decision has been made, and not to adjudicate as part of that decision. Add to these the pressures from the South Glamorgan case and the new Guidelines, both which demand an analysis of degrees of prejudice, and it would seem that the committees should be looking at Tweedie's third or fourth approaches: the Individualist Rights or the Administrative Justice approaches. However, whether the education system can bear the load of 10,000 such appeals each year is very questionable, and one might guess that in practice appeal decisions will be reached after the appeal committee has afforded both parties a less than perfect consideration. It would seem reasonable to ask, therefore, whether the education appeal committees have been set realistic goals.

But this appeals machinery was also intended to oversee the local balance. It was recognized when the Act was being written that central government could not effectively impose a set amount of choice on to so many LEAs which were both educationally autonomous, and geographically and socially different. Whatever system of choice was used it would have to respect local conditions.

However, if the amount of choice was to vary, then there needed to be some controlling oversight since the government was unwilling to give the LEAs 'unlimited power' to decide about parental rights (Boyson, House of Commons Debate; Standing Committee D; 4th Dec. 1979). It was thus decided that the instrument of oversight should be the local statutory education appeal committee which would then take local conditions into account when reaching its LEA-binding decision.

The interviews have clearly demonstrated that many education officers were keenly responsive to the appeal committees' decisions and comments, and that a number of procedures, and to a lesser extent policies, had been adjusted in the light of the committees' comments. But since the appeals themselves can suffer from the problems mentioned, then both the nature and the background to the committees' comments are similarly questionable. If the individual appeals are resolved with imperfect procedures then the information which is fed back to the LEA will potentially lack the finesse required to control the balance properly and effectively.

In essence though, this is hardly a surprising result. In the introduction to this chapter, allocation disputes were described in terms of the conflict of interests between the individual's wishes and the needs of the group. But the resolution of this kind of conflict is a highly sophisticated process as the various demands for natural justice and the equating of degrees of prejudice have demonstrated. With the practical problems of inadequate time, training and independence, and the real difficulties arising from the competition between appellants for a finite number of school places, it seems unreasonable to even expect the committees to meet the goals that have been set for them. It may well be that in the end, parents, schools and LEAs would all be better served if the education appeal committees were given a more modest but more achievable set of goals, but to change their goals would be to change the heart of the 1980 Act.

CHAPTER 8
Conclusion

The 1980 Education Act came into force on 1st October 1980 and applied for the first time to admissions to school in the autumn of 1982. As Chapter 2 indicates, the main factors leading up to the Act were (a) a belief among politicians that there was a growing demand for parental choice; (b) falling rolls and the increasing need to manage places, and (c) the need to amend the unsatisfactory situation arising from a large number of central appeals. The Act had other potential ramifications which included the effects of market forces on schools, a general increase in parents' rights, and a possible strain on LEA resources from having to respect parental preference in the overall management of school places.

The Information for Parental Choice Project set out to investigate the implementation of the new legislation and its implications for LEAs, schools and parents. In considering the impact on LEAs, the fact that the requirements of the Act and subsequent DES regulations were superimposed on existing LEA procedures seems to be crucial. With long-standing admissions procedures already in operation, and with no additional central funding for the Act's implementation, the majority of LEAs seem to have done little more than merely amend or modify their existing systems. Very few were found to have completely reassessed what they were doing. As a consequence of this, the project found that LEAs differed considerably both in their policies towards parental choice and in their administration of school allocation.

It was also found that various features of LEA practice influenced the type and amount of choice available to parents. The most influential of these features included the provision of transport, the discrepancy between a school's capacity and its intended intake figure, the published admissions criteria, the LEA's policy for reducing surplus places and the encouragement of uniformity or diversity amongst its schools. These factors have the potential to exert a greater influence on choice than the existence or absence of catchment areas alone.

The 1980 Act described the necessary content and availability of written information about LEA procedures and individual schools. Such information is obviously necessary if parents are to be able to exercise their rights and to make informed choices about schools. It was found that the LEAs' booklets containing information about their admissions procedures were distributed to all parents and usually, though not always, met the legal requirements. That is not to say, however, that the booklets encouraged the exercising of a choice, nor that they were as informative as they might have been.

Both the provision and distribution of information about individual schools were found to relate closely to the amount of choice available, and in any one area or locality the schools appeared to carry out more or less the same procedures: differences occurred mostly between areas rather than within them. Indeed any school that exceeded the locally agreed level of activity with regards to the provision of information was generally frowned upon by other schools and the LEA and the term 'poaching' was often used. Quite clearly this attitude indicates that individual schools feel that they have certain territorial rights over their local parents. This contrasts with the idea of parents having rights – for example, the right to know more about other schools and the right to ask for the school they prefer.

Even where information about several schools was readily available to the parents the quality of this information was often marred by an LEA requirement for schools to produce a uniform style of brochure; a common practice which rendered it difficult for parents to use the information for comparative purposes.

In Chapter 3 the variation in LEA practice is compared to a continuum of choice with unhindered free choice at one end and tightly restricted catchment areas at the other. The various features of admissions procedures and published information which have been mentioned determine where an authority would be placed along this continuum. However, the project could not discern any straightforward divide between those authorities whose policies supported choice and those whose policies denied it. The problem of there sometimes being only a tenuous link between the purported policy and the actual practice was compounded by a combination of political, social and geographic factors. Added to this was the extent of diversity in school provision. All these factors resulted in the emergence of virtually as many different systems and points on the continuum as there were authorities.

Although the LEAs appeared well spread over the continuum of offered choice, a certain amount of clustering was detectable which enabled three distinct, though not necessarily discrete, groups to be recognized. The first group aimed to offer parents a choice of school from all the schools in the area or LEA: this is the 'optimal choice' group. At the opposite end of the continuum another group seemed to hold community schools and community education as an ideal more important than parental choice and indeed, an ideal which was at times in direct conflict with parental choice. This might be termed the 'minimal choice' group. The third cluster of LEAs, though small, was still important since it combined aspects from both the other two groups and offered an amount of choice within a framework of community education. This might be called the 'hybrid' group.

Providing Optimal Choice

Optimal choice was seen to occur when parents were invited to express a preference for any of the schools in the area or LEA. The project team found 49 such areas which represented 39 per cent of the questionnaire responses. The research further showed that the LEAs' reasons varied from the basic desire to offer choice as a goal in itself, to the intention of using choice to influence school development.

In order to offer choice, with no other associated goals, it would seem that there must be:

1　more than one school to choose from;
2　free, viable transport to any school;
3　information provided on the procedures operated by the LEA; and
4　no LEA or divisional boundary restrictions.

If, however, any educational benefits are to accrue from giving parents such a choice, other aspects must also be taken into consideration. For instance, in order that choice can result in a closer match between the requirements of individual parents and what the schools offer, it is essential that parents have something more substantial than hearsay upon which to base their decisions. Without both good written information and school visits it is difficult to see how there can ever be *informed* choice. Furthermore, the offer of choice might be seen as a hollow exercise if the authority pursued a policy of strict uniformity amongst its schools. If educational benefits are to result from parental choice, there must be a diversity in the education available and the information provided should reflect rather than conceal this diversity.

Similarly, if an authority wishes its schools to respond to parental opinion, it would have to make appropriate arrangements for the schools to receive parents' comments, even, and perhaps especially, when these were somewhat negative. Two important points arise here. First, education officers have often commented that there is little or no educational content in the reasons parents give on their application forms, and therefore that there is no point in passing the reasons on to the schools. Often, however, it was found that parents had been specifically asked to confine their reasons to the published admissions criteria which rarely touched upon educational issues. Whilst it might be difficult to determine admissions solely or even partly on educational grounds, it is difficult to see how schools might benefit from the expression of the parents' views if they are never made aware of them. Secondly, and very much related, in many LEAs it was found that if the reasons were read at all it was often by someone with no educational interest. In numerous LEAs no information about why parents preferred some schools over others reached either the education officers or any of the schools themselves. In the small number of authorities where the admissions decisions for each school were handled by the school's governors the beginnings of a communication channel seemed open. Even so, each school's governors would have to see the parents' reasons for all the local schools, and educational reasons would need to be elicited before schools could respond fully.

The expression of parental choice would seem to lead ultimately to a market forces system. The effect of allowing parents to choose what they believe to be the best school for their child is argued by some to be the most appropriate means of encouraging the 'good' schools to prosper whilst forcing the 'poor' schools to change or close. Supporters of this argument appear to believe that the body of parents, as consumers, should have a direct say in the type of education available and that some of the control held by LEAs should shift towards the parents. Evidence of this practice occurring was seen in the way in which some LEAs coped with falling rolls. These authorities closed or reduced unpopular schools whilst maintaining the size of popular ones. This practice was also reinforced in several of the Secretary of State's refusals to allow popular schools to be reduced significantly.

Providing Minimal Choice

Many LEAs did not support the concept of parental choice, or at least gave it little emphasis above other concerns such as community schooling or the protection of schools which were struggling to maintain or build up their reputation. Despite the fact that these LEAs met the requirements of the 1980 Act and 1981 Regulations, various features in their procedures discouraged or prevented the expression of choice. First, the LEA's general information booklet to parents sometimes set out to dissuade parents from choosing, either by the attitude it conveyed or its failure to provide adequate information. Similarly, by discouraging any diversity between school brochures and/or by requiring that they were only sent to catchment-area parents, the LEA reduced parents' ability to take up possible options. Similar consequences may have arisen from the way open evenings and school talks were organized and publicized – for example, when they were held several months after the choice procedure had been completed.

The actual procedures for expressing a preference can also be made difficult. In some LEAs, if parents wanted a school other than that offered by the authority then they had to request a special form from the primary school or education office, or, more discouraging still, they had to write to the chief education officer giving their reasons for preferring another school. Furthermore some LEAs tried to discourage parents from opting away from their catchment-area school by warning them that in doing so they may lose their child's 'reserved' place at their catchment-area school.

In extreme cases, LEAs loaded their procedures against those parents pursuing a place at an alternative school. Conventionally, parents are informed of their rights to statutory appeal in the general information booklet and again if the LEA rejects their application. However some LEAs ignored this latter stage and effectively reduced the number of parents who might otherwise have appealed by not reminding them of their rights.

There were several arguments put forward by these 'minimal choice' LEAs for blocking or at least not encouraging parental requests. First, many officers took the view that all their schools were equally good and all offered the same opportunities to all pupils. As such they could see no educational grounds for parents preferring one school to another. Some added that by using catchment areas they were able to foster strong curriculum and social links between sectors and thus enhance the educational provision for their pupils. Another argument was that as a consequence of knowing prospective pupil numbers the authority could provide efficient long-term planning for both the LEA and its schools so that the whole authority could benefit from the efficient use of its resources.

Quite clearly, however, schools are not always equal. In some areas where officers acknowledged this they said they still felt justified in upholding a policy of community education in order to protect the rights of all parents. They claimed it was necessary to support unpopular schools so that pupils in these schools were not disadvantaged through a gradual decline in numbers and resources, and some officers also commented that by doing this, local children would be assured of a neighbourhood school in future years. Others have argued that catchment-area policies can be used both to encourage social mixing in schools and to avoid the possibility of schools polarizing in popularity due to the greater mobility of the more affluent parents.

Providing a Hybrid Choice

There were found to be two main types of hybrid choice LEAs. First there were some authorities which always recommended the catchment-area school to parents, whilst also actively encouraging them to express a preference if they so wished. Usually this was facilitated by sending an option form along with the offer of a reserved place. The other type of hybrid LEA asked parents to name the school of their choice, but reminded them which was their local school and pointed out the benefits of inter-sector affiliations and continuity. Both types of hybrid LEA operated at the point where the two previously described systems overlap. Both offered choice quite confidently, whilst also encouraging parents to look at their local school.

The hybrid system seems to offer an attractive compromise since it permits scope for parents to match the school to their requirements (providing the appropriate information is available), and further, it has the benefit of requiring parents to make an active decision as to which school they want – a feature which is often claimed to promote parental commitment to a school. But by its use of a guided choice the hybrid system cannot be thought of as a sensitive indicator of market forces.

Geographical Limitations

Having looked at the three main types of choice offered, there is one further group of LEAs which should be considered. For this group, geographic features predominated above all else. Typically these LEAs consisted of sparsely populated rural areas with small towns that could rarely support more than one secondary school. Choice of school was totally overwhelmed by the practical consideration of journey time, even where the parents or the LEA could pay for transport to alternative schools. In one instance the choice that was offered to a group of parents was described to the project as being between a comprehensive day school with a jorurney of an hour or more in a fast bus, or weekly boarding. These LEAs or areas cannot lie on the continuum simply because they have no means of offering any choice.

Parents' Responses

The project team asked similar or identical questions of parents in four very different authorities. The information sought was about the parents themselves, their children, their perceptions of how much choice they had been offered, and the type of information which had been available and used when making their choices. The schools chosen were not in any way intended to be a representative cross-section of schools in general and no attempt has been made to extrapolate to the national context. However, they have served to demonstrate that parents were influenced by very localized issues when choosing schools and that even within one LEA, not all parents wanted the same from their child's school. Thus although across the 18 schools there was a tendency for 'educational standards and academic record' to emerge as one of the most important single reasons for choosing a school, there was considerable variation in the strength of this feeling, and the other reasons were more localized still; often reflecting a school's specific image.

Another feature which emerged from the parents' responses was the link between the amount of information they used, the nature of their jobs and the time they spent at school themselves. The use of information seems clearly linked to elements of social class and by the amount of choice parents perceived to be available. It seems that the less choice parents perceived they had, the fewer of them were involved in any of the pre-choice activities. On the other hand, where all parents were invited to attend parents' evenings or talks, and where published information was readily available, parents' responses demonstrated their willingness to become involved and make the most of the information available to them. This willingness was represented in all strata of society, though more so among those with white collar jobs.

Between the four authorities, the percentage of parents who felt that they had been given a choice ranged from 26 to 84 per cent. However, despite this discrepancy, it was salutary to discover that similar percentages of parents from each of the LEAs had known which school they wanted over a year earlier (71 per cent on average) and approximately 86 per cent of all those parents who had known which school they wanted eventually secured a place for their child at that school. However, these last two figures are potentially misleading since we still do not know how much the parents' choice had been conditioned by the LEA's arrangements and in turn how these arrangements were dependent upon how long the 1980 Act has been in force.

One of the problems the research has been aware of is that the Act has only been in operation since 1982 and that it may well be a number of years before its full implications are realized by the parents and accepted by the authorities. Certainly in respect of appeals the interpretation of parents' rights is evolving rapidly and the balance between the parent's individual wishes and the broader needs of society is still moving towards the parent. As such, whilst appeal committees continue to argue what is meant by a 'full' school and to reinterpret their LEA's criteria, the issue of choice still must always come face to face with the problem of numbers. In doing so though it may be overshadowing the more important issues of quality.

In looking back to the mid- to late seventies, when central government was embarrassed by the large numbers of central appeals, the issue at stake was not that parents as a whole wanted choice so much as that individual parents wanted to gain access to their preferred schools. These parents were trying to improve their child's education by sending him or her to the school they felt would give the best education as they saw it. The whole purpose of being able to choose a school was to improve education at the individual level. What needs to be asked now is whether the progression from the concept of 'choice for a few' to 'choice for all' could actually lead to improved educational provision, and what would be necessary to facilitate its operation.

The research has clearly shown that the majority of LEAs are operating a system which meets the legal requirements of the 1980 Education Act. However, the fact that the concept which started out as *parental choice* was finally phrased in the Act as the right to *express a preference* means that 'choice for all' is still a long way off. Indeed it appears that many parents have had their hopes raised by popular misuse of the word 'choice', only to be disappointed by LEA officers who feel the need to constantly reiterate the terminology of the legislation, i.e. preference. While the Act has stimulated much lively debate and interest as to the rights and wrongs of choice, it does not appear to have altered the state of play significantly. Only time will tell if the balance between parents and LEAs has really shifted to any extent and, if so, whether it will bring about any beneficial changes to schools.

Appendix

Appendix 2.1:   Education Act 1980, section 6

(1)   Every local education authority shall make arrangements for enabling the parent of a child in the area of the authority to express a preference as to the school at which he wishes education to be provided for his child in the exercise of the authority's functions and to give reasons for his preference.

(2)   Subject to subsection (3) below, it shall be the duty of a local education authority and of the governors of a county voluntary school to comply with any preference expressed in accordance with the arrangements.

(3)   The duty imposed by subsection (2) above does not apply –
   (*a*)   if compliance with the preference would prejudice the provision of efficient education or the efficient use of resources;
   (*b*)   if the preferred school is an aided or special agreement school and compliance with the preference would be incompatible with any arrangements between the governors and the local education authority in respect of the admission of pupils to the school; or
   (*c*)   if the arrangements for admission to the preferred school are based wholly or partly on selection by reference to ability or aptitude and compliance with the preference would be incompatible with selection under the arrangements.

(4)   Where the arrangements for the admission of pupils to a school maintained by a local education authority provide for applications for admission to be made to, or to a person acting on behalf of, the governors of the school, a parent who makes such an application shall be regarded for the purposes of subsection (2)

above as having expressed a preference for that school in accordance with arrangements made under subsection (1) above.

(5)   The duty imposed by subsection (2) above in relation to a preference expressed in accordance with arrangements made under subsection (1) above shall apply also in relation to –

  (*a*)   any application for the admission to a school maintained by a local education authority of a child who is not in the area of the authority; and

  (*b*)   any application made as mentioned in section 10(3) or 11(1) below;

and reference in subsection (3) above to a preference and a preferred school shall be construed accordingly.

Appendix 2.2: Education Act 1980, section 7

(1)   Every local education authority shall make arrangements for enabling the parent of a child to appeal against –
- (*a*)   any decision made by or on behalf of the authority as to the school at which education is to be provided for the child in the exercise of the authority's functions; and
- (*b*)   any decision made by or on behalf of the governors of a county or controlled school maintained by the authority refusing the child admission to such a school.

(2)   The governors of every aided or special agreement school shall make arrangements for enabling the parent of a child to appeal against any decision made by or on behalf of the governors refusing the child admission to the school.

(3)   Joint arrangements may be made under section (2) above by the governors of two or more aided or special agreement schools maintained by the same local education authority.

(4)   Any appeal by virtue of this section shall be to an appeal committee constituted in accordance with Part 1 of Schedule 2 to this Act; and Part II of that Schedule shall have effect in relation to the procedure on any such appeal.

(5)   The decision of an appeal committee on any such appeal shall be binding on the local education authority or governors by or on whose behalf the decision under appeal was made and, in the case of a decision made by or on behalf of a local education authority, on the governors of any county or controlled school at which the committee determines that a place should be offered to the child in question.

(6)   In paragraph 6 of Schedule 1 to the Tribunals and Inquiries Act 1971 (tribunals under direct supervision of the Council on Tribunals) after '6', there shall be inserted '(*a*)' and at the end there shall be inserted –
- '(*b*)   appeal committees constituted in accordance with Part 1 of Schedule 2 to the Education Act 1980 (c.20)'.

and in section 13(1) of the Act for '6' there shall be substituted '6(*a*)'.

(7)   In section 25 of the Local Government Act 1974 (authorities subject to investigation by Local Commissioner) after subsection (4) there shall be inserted –

'(5)   Any reference to an authority to which this Part of this Act applies also includes a reference to any appeal committee constituted in accordance with paragraph 1 of Schedule 2 to the Education Act 1980.'

Appendix 2.3: Education Act 1980, section 8

(1)   Every local education authority shall, for each school year, publish particulars of –
  (*a*)   the arrangements for the admission of pupils to schools maintained by the authority, other than aided or special agreement schools;
  (*b*)   the authority's arrangements for the provision of education at schools maintained by another local education authority; and
  (*c*)   the arrangements made by the authority under section 6(1) and 7(1) above.

(2)   The governors of every aided or special agreement school shall, for each school year, publish particulars of –
  (*a*)   the arrangements for the admission of pupils to the school; and
  (*b*)   the arrangements made by them under section 7(2) above.

(3)   The particulars to be published under subsections (1)(*a*) and (2)(*a*) above shall include particulars of –
  (*a*)   the number of pupils that it is intended to admit in each school year to each school to which the arrangements relate, being pupils in the age group in which pupils are normally admitted or, if there is more than one such group, in each such group;
  (*b*)   the respective admission functions of the local education authority and the governors;
  (*c*)   the policy followed in deciding admissions;
  (*d*)   the arrangements made in respect of pupils not belonging to the area of the local education authority.

(4)   The particulars to be published under subsection (1)(*b*) above shall include particulars of –
  (*a*)   the criteria for offering places at schools not maintained by a local education authority;
  (*b*)   the names of, and number of places at, any such schools in respect of which the authority have standing arrangements.

(5) Every local education authority shall, as respects each school maintained by them other than an aided or special agreement school, and the governors of every aided or special agreement school shall, as respects that school, publish –

(*a*)   such information as may be required by regulations made by the Secretary of State; and

(*b*)   such other information, if any, as the authority or governors think fit,

and every local education authority shall also publish such information as may be so required with respect to their policy and arrangements in respect of any matter relating to primary or secondary education in their area.

(6) The local education authority by whom an aided or special agreement school is maintained may, with the agreement of the governors of the school, publish on their behalf the particulars or information relating to the school referred to in subsection (2) or (5) above.

(7) References in this section to publication are references to publication at such time or times and in such manner as may be required by regulations made by the Secretary of State.

Appendix 2.4: Education Act 1980, Schedule 2

Part II Procedure

5. An appeal shall be by notice in writing setting out the grounds on which it is made.

6. An appeal committee shall afford the appellant an opportunity of appearing and making oral representations and may allow the appellant to be accompanied by a friend or to be represented.

7. The matters to be taken into account by an appeal committee in considering an appeal shall include –
   (*a*)   any preference expressed by the appellant in respect of the child as mentioned in section 6 of this Act; and
   (*b*)   the arrangements for the admission of pupils published by the local education authority or the governors under section 8 of this Act.

8. In the event of disagreement between the members of an appeal committee the appeal under consideration shall be decided by a simple majority of the votes cast and in the case of an equality of votes the chairman of the committee shall have a second or casting vote.

9. The decision of an appeal committee and the grounds on which it is made shall be communicated by the committee in writing to –
   (*a*)   the appellant and the local education authority, and
   (*b*)   in the case of an appeal to an appeal committee constituted in accordance with paragraph 2 or 3 above, to the governors by or on whose behalf the decision appealed against was made.

10. Appeals pursuant to arrangements made under section 7 of this Act shall be heard in private except when otherwise directed by the authority or governors by whom the arrangements are made but, without prejudice to paragraph 6 above, a number of the local education authority may attend as an observer any hearing of an appeal by an appeal committee constituted in accordance with

paragraph 1 above, and a member of the Council on Tribunals may attend as an observer any meeting of any appeal committee at which an appeal is considered.

11.   Subject to paragraphs 5 to 10 above, all matters relating to the procedure on appeals pursuant to arrangements made under section 7 of this Act, including the time within which they are to be brought, shall be determined by the authority or governors by whom the arrangements are made; and neither section 106 of the Local Government Act 1972 nor paragraph 44 of Schedule 12 to that Act (procedure of committees of local authorities) shall apply to an appeal committee constituted in accordance with paragraph 1 above.

Appendix 3.1

A certain amount of supporting material is available from the authors upon request. Please write to them at the National Foundation for Educational Research, The Mere, Upton Park, Slough, Berks., specifying which items are required.

A Table showing the size of the administrative areas used in 1984 survey: (1) by intake numbers; (2) by numbers of schools.

B The full version of the Parents' Questionnaire – IPC 1984.

C The main aspects which were most important to parents when choosing a school, by school.

D Influence on the numbers of each type of reason given by parents by their terminal-education ages by sex.

E Influence on the numbers of parents giving the different combinations of reason-types by the parents' own education by sex.

Appendix: Table 5.1:   Classification of things most important to parents when choosing a school – question MS7

(A: process   B: product   C: geography   D: other)

	'EDUCATIONAL' CLASSIFICATION (Derived from open-ended responses)	percentage of parents giving reason
	GEOGRAPHIC	
C	Short distance/close (inc. locality = nearness)	27.7
C	Easy to get to/accessible/safe journey	9.4
C	Easy travelling/transport free or provided	7.5
*A/B	Best school in area (emphasis on area)	0.1
	ACADEMIC	
*A/B	Good reputation/well recommended – vague but positive	16.9
B	Good standards of education/exam results/ academic record	52.1
A	Flexible curriculum to maximize child's potential	1.7
A	Wide choice of subjects/options – broad curriculum	14.8
B	High standards in the arts/music/culture	0.9
B	High standards in sports/PE	1.1
B	High standards in craft subjects	†0.0
B	High standards in science/maths	0.1
A	Supportive of slow learners: availability of remedial help	1.3
A	High university entrance rate/encourages FE/ 6th-form	1.7
A	Traditional approach	0.8
A	Good opportunities/high chances of achievement	1.8

A	Academic atmosphere/emphasis on GCE more than CSE	2.9
A	Curriculum – favourable comments in general	2.5

FACILITIES

A	Good facilities – unspecified	11.8
A	Good facilities – science/languages/maths	0.6
A	Good facilities – arts/music including has an orchestra	0.9
A	Good facilities – sports, etc.	4.4
A	Good facilities – crafts, etc.	0.3
A	Modern, up-to-date equipment	1.2
A	Good buildings (and playing fields)	1.3
A	All on one site	†0.0
A	School not too large/school size	3.7
A	Class-size, pupil/teacher ratios	1.6

PASTORAL REASONS

A	Good discipline	38.0
A	Uniform	6.8
A	Children's behaviour and appearance good	4.7
A	Happy, caring atmosphere – pleasant place	6.6
A	Good settling-in procedures	0.3
A	Many activities/hobbies/clubs	5.4
A	Bright and tidy school: clean	0.9
A	Lively interests	†0.0
A	A good system of monitoring child's progress	0.3
A	Denominational	7.5
A	Moral emphasis – including 'Christian ethic'	1.9
A	Non-denominational	0.2
A	Encourages initiative/treats children as individuals	0.9
A	Respect and cooperation between teachers and pupils	0.3
A	Relaxed discipline	0.3

SCHOOL TYPE

A	Co-educational	3.0
A	Single-sex (boys only or girls only) and including single-sex teaching for part of school	6.3
A	Comprehensive	1.4
A	Selective or grammar	1.4
A	Retains selective ethos though no longer grammar school	†0.0
A	Split-age school, i.e. junior and senior	0.2
A	Split-site school therefore not too large	0.3
A	Locality of school, i.e. in a good or nice area	1.3
A	1st–6th form inclusive/has 6th form/ good 6th form	1.2
A	Streaming	1.9
A	Modern teaching methods	0.5
A	Mixed ability in 1st year	0.1
A	A school that is *not* too academic	†0.0
A	Homework (i.e. lots)	0.6
A	Thorough homework organization	0.3

TEACHER AND HEAD ATTRIBUTES

A	Teachers accessible to pupils/ good relationship	2.3
A	Teachers accessible to parents/open evenings	1.4
A	Communication with parents	0.9
A	Caring staff/understanding teaching/friendly teachers	6.2
A	Attitude of staff including positive attitude/ dedicated	4.1
A	Good teacher/parent relationship	1.5
A	A stable staff	0.4
A	The staff run the school well/well organized or well run	1.1
A	Good head with a supportive staff	2.1
A	Competent teaching/quality of staff	5.8
A	The staff	0.4

RECORDING AGENTS

D	Parents of children already there	0.8
D	Recommended by other parents	1.0
D	Popular school (no agent)	0.2
D	Parent(s) work at school	0.2
D	Recommended by present pupils	0.9
D	Recommendations of junior school headteacher	0.4
D	Other schools not recommended	0.1
D	Recommendation by primary school teachers	†0.0
D	Past pupils who now have good careers	†0.0
A	Liked what we saw on open evening/visit to school	0.7
A	Knowing children at the school who are doing well	†0.0

CHILD AND FAMILY REASONS

A	Child wants to go there	8.2
D	Child recommends it	0.9
D	Child's friends will be going there	6.7
D	Siblings already there or been there, i.e. recommendation	6.5
D	Other family members there	0.4
A	Where child would be happy	7.7
A	Where parents can become involved	0.6
D	Parent(s) went there	0.7
A	Have confidence in the school	0.2
A	Best for child or welfare of child	0.5
A	Compatibility of parent and school aims or philosophy	0.5
A	Suited to child's needs academically	4.2

OTHER SOMEWHAT UNCOMMON REASONS

A	Equal opportunities for boys and girls	0.2
A	Not over-mixed racially/ethnic mix	†0.0
A	Racial compatibility with other children going there	0.1
D	Economical (e.g. siblings and second-hand uniforms)	0.1
D	Reasons associated with PTA	0.3
D	Extremely obscure reasons, in total. . .	12.5

Total percentage of reasons given:	342.5%

Overall 2245 parents gave 7689 useful reasons, i.e. an average of 3.4 reasons for each of these parents.
18.1 per cent of the 2740 parents returning questionnaires omitted this question.

* These two reasons can be taken as either process or product.

† A small number of parents gave each of these reasons, but not enough to register to one decimal place here.

Appendix: Table 6.1: Reasons given by those Shiretown parents who said that they felt they had had no choice

	Hollybush	Oaklands	Roseview	Aldertree
	%	%	%	%
Assumed children automatically went to catchment-area school	11	6	16	16
Only one school offered – there was no choice	21	29	13	22
Choice limited by transport (bus services/passes, etc.)	7	6	19	17
Told by head/staff of primary school that they had to attend the school	2	14	0	4
No reasons given	59	44	52	41
Total Percentage	100	99	100	100
Number of parents	160	167	67	193

Appendix: Table 6.2:   Who the parents consulted about choice of school (Schools arranged in descending order of perceived choice within LEA)

| | SHIRETOWN | | | | SEATOWN | | | | |
	Oaklands	Roseview	Hollybush	Aldertree	Girls' High	St Paul's	Newcrest	Hawthorn	Steepleton
	%	%	%	%	%	%	%	%	%
Nobody	26	27	37	50	10	14	24	23	29
Junior/primary school head	20	23	18	15	64	34	17	23	23
Junior/primary school staff	30	26	25	19	52	33	28	29	29
Secondary school head(s)	16	15	13	6	10	37	17	19	10
Secondary school staff	12	11	9	5	13	10	11	16	7
Parents of other children at secondary school	43	41	39	26	62	50	45	44	39
Other parents with 11-year-olds	22	37	24	22	48	33	29	35	29
Their 11-year-old child	50	44	41	24	73	55	52	52	55
Family/friends/ neighbours	37	33	35	22	49	43	39	36	36
TOTAL	230	230	204	139	371	295	238	254	228

(Parents could give more than one response)

Appendix: Table 6.2 (contd)

	NORTHTOWN					SOUTHBOROUGH			
	Ashfield Sec. Mod.	Birchtree Sec. Mod.	Northtown High School	Riverview Comprehensive	Cattleford Sec. Mod.	London Bridge	All Saints	Tower Bridge	Richmond Bridge
Nobody	% 36	% 35	% 17	% 28	% 49	% 21	% 21	% 12	% 17
Junior/primary school head	15	8	42	22	20	30	36	29	26
Secondary school head(s)	3	4	6	6	8	6	24	25	26
Secondary school staff	4	3	7	10	5	11	5	12	4
Parents of other children at secondary school	17	26	31	38	19	9	12	13	13
Other parents with 11-year-olds	14	23	31	22	12	28	24	45	34
Their 11-year-old child	55	49	63	38	31	11	7	28	32
Family/friends/ neighbours	50	35	36	25	25	36	29	41	38
TOTAL	158	148	216	161	120	131	137	193	173

(Parents could give more than one response)

Appendix: Table 6.3: **'If you visited one or more schools before you had to choose, how useful did you find the school visits when choosing a school?'**

The visits were . . .	Hollybush	Oaklands	Roseview	Aldertree
	%	%	%	%
. . . most useful in choosing a school	25	46	26	20
. . . only confirmed what you already felt	61	44	58	59
. . . were of little use in choosing a school	13	10	16	23

Appendix: Table 6.4:   Number of school brochures seen, by school
(The schools are arranged in descending order of perceived choice within LEA)

'How many different school brochures did you see before choice?'

| | SHIRETOWN LEA | | | | SEATOWN LEA | | | | |
	Oaklands	Roseview	Hollybush	Aldertree	Girls High	St Paul's	Newcrest	Hawthorn	Steepleton
	%	%	%	%	%	%	%	%	%
none	41	32	53	55	41	31	50	47	45
one	43	49	31	34	19	22	37	40	31
two	9	9	7	3	17	35	9	8	18
three or more	4	4	5	1	21	12	3	3	4
seen at least one	56	62	43	38	57	69	49	51	53

| | NORTHTOWN LEA | | | | | SOUTHBOROUGH LEA | | | |
	Ashfield	Birchtree	Northtown	Riverview	Cattleford	London Bridge	All Saints'	Tower Bridge	Richmond Bridge
	%	%	%	%	%	%	%	%	%
none	65	60	61	45	60	40	31	38	45
one	23	31	20	36	23	40	33	25	21
two	8	8	9	10	8	4	19	17	21
three or more	1	1	7	3	2	13	10	16	11
seen at least one	32	40	36	49	33	57	62	58	53

Appendix: Table 6.5:   The numbers of school exam results seen by parents, by school.
(The schools are arranged in descending order of perceived choice within each LEA)

'How many schools' examination results did you see before you had to make your choice?'

| | SHIRETOWN LEA | | | | SEATOWN LEA | | | | |
	Oaklands	Roseview	Hollybush	Aldertree	Girls High	St Paul's	Newcrest	Hawthorn	Steepleton
	%	%	%	%	%	%	%	%	%
none	64	51	54	76	48	54	47	67	81
one	9	14	7	5	19	24	30	23	8
two	12	9	9	4	18	13	11	5	6
three or more	12	15	24	7	12	5	8	2	2
seen at least one	33	38	40	16	49	42	49	30	16

| | NORTHTOWN LEA | | | | | SOUTHBOROUGH LEA | | | |
	Ashfield	Birchtree	Northtown	Riverview	Cattleford	London Bridge	All Saints'	Tower Bridge	Richmond Bridge
	%	%	%	%	%	%	%	%	%
none	89	82	62	57	71	64	50	50	62
one	5	8	12	23	12	6	17	12	15
two	2	8	11	6	5	13	17	8	11
three or more	1	3	12	6	2	13	12	20	13
seen at least one	8	19	35	35	19	32	46	40	39

Appendix: Table 7.1: Numbers and percentages of parents getting first choice at the initial allocation stages, England and Wales: information supplied by education officers in response to the project's questionnaire: See Appendix 3.1 for more detail

	1983	1984
No. of transferring pupils in free choice areas[1]	145,501	137,400
No. of transferring pupils in catchment areas[1]	289,812	247,781
Total[2] no. of transferring pupils	435,313	385,181
% parents *not* gaining 1st choice in free choice areas	7.8% (N=11,385)	9.4% (N=12,978)
%parents *not* accepting catchment area school[3]	7.6% (N=22,107)	9.0% (N=22,254)

Notes
1. See Chapter 3 for definitions.
2. These figures include pupils of different ages, i.e. between 10 and 14 years and they correspond to approximately 63% of the total population of 11-year-olds in England and Wales for both years.
3. Many catchment-area LEAs used the percentage of parents who did *not* request another school, as the percentage gaining their 1st choice. As this is the only statistic available which might give any indication of the proportion gaining their first choice we have included it here with a reservation concerning the implicit assumption.

References I

Legislation Referred to in Text

Parliamentary Acts

Education Act 1944
Education Act 1976
Education Act 1979
Education Act 1980
London Government Act 1963

Parliamentary Bills

1943 Education Bill (to become 1944 Education Act)
1970 Education Bill No. 91 (references appear in the literature to a
               second Labour Bill in this year but it was
               never published)
1976 Education (Parents' Charter) Bill
1978 Education Bill
1979 Education Bill (to become 1979 Education Act)
1979 Education (No. 2) Bill (to become 1980 Education Act)

*Board of Education, Ministry of Education and DES Papers,
Circulars and Instruments*

Board of Education (1943)   Educational Reconstruction Cmnd.
                                6458 (Reprinted 1959), London.
Ministry of Education(1945)   Administrative Memorandum
                                No.63(1st June 1945). Transport of
                                Pupils to School.
                                London: Ministry of Education.

Ministry of Education(1946) Choice of Schools, Circular 83
(14th Jan. 1946).
London: Ministry of Education.
Ministry of Education(1950) Choice of Schools, Manual of
Guidance Schools No. 1, London.
DES (1965) Circular 10/65. London: HMSO.
DES (1970) Unpublished Green Paper
(referred to but never located!)
DES (1976) Draft Circular to LEAs and
Governors and Managers of
Voluntary Schools. Admission of
Children to Schools of Their
Parents' Choice.
DES (1977A) Education in Schools.
A Consultative Document
DES (1977B) Admission of Children to Schools
of their Parents' Choice.
London: DES.
Consultation Paper, October 1977.
DES (1981A) Circular 1/81 Education Act 1980
Admission to Schools.
London: DES.
DES (1981B) Circular 2/81
Falling Rolls and Surplus Places.
London: DES.
DES (1981C) Education (School Information)
Regulations 1981. London: DES

R. v. *South Glamorgan Appeals Committee, ex parte Dafydd Evans*,
10th May 1984.
Available from the shorthand notes of Marten Walsh Chever Ltd.,
London EC4Y 8BH.

References II

ASSOCIATION OF COUNTY COUNCILS (ACC) (1985). *Code of Practice as to the Constitution and Procedures of Appeal Committees Established under the Education Act 1980.* London: ACC.

ASSOCIATION OF METROPOLITAN AUTHORITIES (AMA) (1985). *Code of Practice as to the Constitution and Procedures of Appeal Committees Established under the Education Act 1980.* London: AMA.

ATHERTON, G. (1979). *Reaching Out to Parents.* Glasgow: Scottish Consumer Council.

ATHERTON, G. (1982). *The Book of the School: A Study of Scottish School Handbooks Issued to Pupils and Their Parents.* Glasgow: Scottish Consumer Council.

BASTIANI, J. (Ed) (1978). *Written Communication Between Home and School.* Nottingham: University of Nottingham School of Education.

BERLINER, W. (1983). 'School choice scheme hits trouble' *The Guardian,* 12th August.

BOYSON, R. (1970). 'Appraisal'. In: *Education a Framework for Choice* (2nd Edition). London: Institute of Economic Affairs.

BULL, D. (1980). 'School admissions: a new appeals procedure', *Journal of Social Welfare Law,* 209–233.

BULL, D. (1985). 'Monitoring education appeals: local ombudsmen lead the way', *Journal of Social Welfare Law,* July, 184–226.

BULL, D. (1986). 'Tameside: prospectively "reasonable"; retrospectively "maladministration", *Journal of Social Welfare Law* (forthcoming).

CONSERVATIVE PARTY (1974A). *Firm Action for a Fair Britain.* The Conservative Manifesto. London: Conservative Central Office.

CONSERVATIVE PARTY (1974B). *Putting Britain First: A National Policy from the Conservatives.* London: Conservative Central Office.

ELLIOTT, J., BRIDGES, D., GIBSON, R. and NIAS, J. (1981). *School Accountability.* The SSRC Cambridge Accountability Project. London: Grant McIntyre.

FLEW, A. (1983). *Power to the People.* London: Centre for Policy Studies.

FOWLER, G. (1979). 'The Accountability of Ministers'. In: LELLO, J. (Ed) *Accountability in Education.* London: Ward Lock Education.

FRIEDMAN, M. and FRIEDMAN, R. (1981). *Free to Choose.* New York: Avon Nonfic.

JOSEPH, K. (1982). '99th Conservative Party Conference Address'. Reported in *Education,* 8th October 1982, p. 265.

KENT COUNTY COUNCIL (1978). *Education Vouchers in Kent.* Maidstone: Kent County Council.

LABOUR PARTY (1972). *Labour's Programme for Britain*. London: The Labour Party.

LELLO, J. (Ed) (1979). *Accountability in Education*. London: Ward Lock Education.

MEREDITH, P. (1981). 'Executive discretion and choice of secondary school', *Public Law*, Spring 1981, p. 52.

MIDDLETON, N. and WEITZMAN, S. (1976). *A Place for Everyone: A History of State Education from the End of the 18th Century to the 1970s*. London: Victor Gollancz.

MILL, J.S. (1859). 'On Liberty'. In: WARNOCK, M. (Ed) (1962) *Utilitarianism: John Stuart Mill*. London: Fontana.

MONK, D. (1978). *Social Grading on the National Readership Survey*. London: Joint Industry Committee for National Readership Surveys.

NEWELL, P. (1983). '1981 Act: No Parents' Charter on Choice Appeals', *Where*, 185. February 1983.

OLDMEADOW, E. (1944). 'Francis Cardinal Bourne'. Vol II, Chap. 32, in *Education a Framework for Choice* (1970). London: Institute for Economic Affairs.

PASSMORE, B. (1983). 'Long hot summer of parental discontent', *Times Ed. Supp.*, 19th Aug. 1983.

PLEWIS, I., GRAY, J., FOGELMAN, K., MORTIMORE, P. and BYFORD, D. (1981). *Publishing School Examination Results: A Discussion*, Bedford Way Papers. London: University of London Institute of Education.

STILLMAN, A.B. and MAYCHELL, K. (1984). *School to School: LEA and Teacher Involvement in Educational Continuity*. Windsor: NFER-NELSON.

SUGARMAN, D. (1979). 'How parental choice could enhance school power', *Education*, 153, p. 487. 17/27 April 1979.

ST JOHN STEVAS, N. (1977). *Better Schools For All*. London: Conservative Political Centre.

TAYLOR, F. (1980). *School Prospectus Planning Kit*. London: Advisory Centre for Education.

TWEEDIE, J. (1986). 'Rights in social programs: the case of parental choice of school', *Public Law* (forthcoming).

WILLIAMS, S. (1985). Interview with Jack Tweedie and Andy Stillman. Not published.